PROJECT LEADERSHIP

Project Leadership
Second Edition

Wendy Briner, Colin Hastings and Michael Geddes

Gower

Published by
Gower Publishing Limited
Gower House
Croft Road
Aldershot
Hampshire GU11 3HR
England

Gower
Old Post Road
Brookfield
Vermont 05036
USA

Reprinted 1997

Wendy Briner, Colin Hastings and Michael Geddes have asserted their right under the Copyright, Designs and Patents Act 1988 to be identified as the authors of this work.

British Library Cataloguing in Publication Data

Briner, Wendy
 Project Leadership. – 2Rev.ed
 I. Title
 657.404

   ISBN 0–566–07714–0 Hardback
        0–566–07785–X Paperback

Library of Congress Cataloging-in-Publication Data

Briner, Wendy.
    Project leadership / Wendy Briner, Colin Hastings, and Michael
  Geddes. — 2nd ed.
      p. cm.
    Includes index.
    ISBN 0–566–07714–0 (hardback)
    1. Industrial project management. 2. Leadership. I. Hastings,
  Colin. II. Geddes, Michael. III. Title.
  HD69.P75B75 1995
  658.4'04—dd20   95–30772
                                                                   CIP

Typeset in Helvetica and Century Old Style by Bournemouth Colour Press and printed in Great Britain by Biddles Ltd, Guildford.

Contents

List of figures

Preface

This book is not about project management as most people understand the term. It is about the rapidly growing new specialism of project leadership in organizations.

The world of traditional project management is evolving rapidly in two fundamental ways. Firstly it is moving away from a preoccupation with project planning and control tools as the keys to success, and towards the management of people and their performance. Secondly it is moving away from a preoccupation with complex construction projects towards a wider appreciation of the diversity of 'projects' that are mushrooming within organizations.

The new ways in which organizations are using projects as mechanisms for managing innovation and change, or making things happen fast, have resulted in the rapid rise in importance of a new role – that of the project leader. Few people will bear that title; they are more likely to be called New Product Development Manager, Computer Installation Co-ordinator or Exhibitions Manager, and so on. Many will not have titles at all, such as the person evaluating and preparing for a new acquisition, or the person appointed to co-ordinate a move to new offices.

Over the last ten years we have been concerned to identify the essential attributes of the effective project leader. How do the successful ones make things happen in practice, often in situations of great uncertainty, complexity and organizational change? Our learning grew originally out of the activities of the specialist teamworking research and consultancy unit we founded at Ashridge Management College. That early work was summarized in a now standard text on high-performing teams: *Superteams: Building Organisational Success Through High Performing Teams*, published by HarperCollins in 1986. Since then, with two other ex-Ashridge colleagues, we have formed our own consulting business, New Organisation Consulting. Later work which shows the growing importance of the project way of working in emerging new forms of organization is pulled together in another book: *The New Organization: Growing the Culture of Organizational Networking*, published by McGraw-Hill in 1993. During this time we have been working a great deal with the new breed of project leaders, both in consultancy assignments and in the special course we developed to meet their training needs entitled 'Leading Projects Effectively'. We have also looked at the many ways in which projects of different types are being used within organizations as diverse as manufacturing, financial services, retail organizations, an opera company, television, the lifeboat service and a political party.

This revised edition says little about the traditional project management techniques because many of the new project leaders find them inappropriate or limited in application. It concentrates instead on the skills, awareness and understanding deployed by project leaders operating successfully in a wide range of organizational and project settings. We have tried to distil their experience, make sense of it, and present it in a form that will provide both conceptual clarity and practical payoff for the growing number of people who find themselves permanently or occasionally in project leadership roles.

The book begins by explaining why the concept of project teams is being adopted so enthusiastically in modern organizations.

In Part I 'The project leader' we chart the territory of the project leader's role and its associated skills and competence requirement in some detail. We also introduce the important concept of the project spectrum, a way of describing the range of fundamentally different project types that we now encounter in organizations, each of which requires a tailored leadership approach.

Part II 'Preparing the ground' demonstrates the importance of understanding and managing the fundamental organizational realities within which the project will be judged to have succeeded or failed. Chapters on the big picture, managing the sponsor and the process of scoping cover these aspects.

Part III 'Managing the project' covers the practicalities of making it happen, from project start-up, through marketing its benefits, to keeping it and the team on track, and finally to handing over and winding up.

Part IV 'Action summary' provides chapter summaries of key points and key questions for the reader, together with key references.

We know that the rapidly growing project leadership role is and will be of fundamental importance to all organizations. It is a pivotal integrating role that is both exceedingly demanding and also very rewarding personally and in performance terms when skilfully executed. Dumping people unprepared into such roles is an almost certain recipe for failure. This book demonstrates our cumulative experience of how we have helped organizations to make the project way of working work for them.

May 1995

Wendy Briner
Colin Hastings
New Organisation Consulting
P O Box 2804
London NW11 7LQ
England

Acknowledgements

First edition

Edgar Wille, who provided us with much valuable criticism and who, single-handed, fashioned our different styles and contributions into a consistent whole.

Karen Watts, Deborah Barrow, Liz Tabel and Liz Hoare, who politely and good-humouredly deciphered our scribbles and masterfully manipulated the word processor through many drafts, re-drafts, last-but-one drafts, pre-final versions and … wait for it … final versions!

Our colleagues in Ashridge Teamworking Services, David Pearce, Peter Bixby, Julia Pokora, Frank Tyrrell and Sally Klewin, who have in many ways contributed to, and influenced, our thinking.

Our consultancy clients, research collaborators and course members, who are all out there in the jungle 'doing it'.

To each other, for sticking with it.

Second edition

Isobel Exell and Jane Boddington, for their wizardry in translating our cutting and pasting into legible text.

Our colleague, Julia Pokora, in New Organisation Consulting, for permission to use extracts of articles she has written in our regular series in *Project Manager Today.*

WB, CH, MG

Introduction
The brave new world of project management

Introduction: The brave new world of project management

John Kingsley had a disaster on his hands. He'd worked in a construction company all his life as a project manager. There was nothing he didn't know about getting buildings up on time, within budget and to the technical spec. Three years ago he'd wanted a change and taken a new job as Co-ordinator of New Stores Development with a large high street retailing group and life had been nothing but hassle ever since. 'They make it so complicated here,' he said, '*Everyone* wants their say; the Merchandising people, the Finance Director, the Distribution people ... even Personnel think they have a right to dictate to me.' To make things more difficult, John didn't control his own construction team any longer – there were subcontractors whom he thought were appalling, but they'd always done the Group's new stores. And the Architect and Interior Designers – what a crowd! They could never make up their minds what they wanted. The last straw was a telephone call from the recently appointed Store Manager saying did he not realize the impact on the bottom line, and their reputation, if the previously announced store opening had to be delayed by three weeks; then there was a message asking John to make sure he attended a meeting with the Managing Director that afternoon!

Consider another case where Liz Jones, working for a computer systems company, was asked to take over a prestige project to introduce a computerized typesetting and layout facility for a national newspaper. The project was already in mid-cycle. The client organization, however, had demanded the replacement of the existing project team because its key managers were not being fully kept in touch with progress. In this case, the challenge facing Liz was how to manage:

- the expectations of senior management in her own organization – who regarded the project as vital to the organization's reputation and commercial future
- the needs of senior management in the client organization – who were dissatisfied with progress and felt excluded from the planning process
- the demands of technical staff in the client organization – who had specific requirements from the system being introduced which were not being met

- the problem of assembling a new team which, for political reasons, needed to include some members of its de-motivated predecessor
- the difficulties of keeping the members of this team in touch with each other when it included both American and European advisers
- the delicate exercise of negotiating additional financial resources when the project was already badly over budget.

Today's project management

Thousands of project leaders, project managers and project co-ordinators will be familiar with the kinds of situation described above. Although project management has traditionally been found mainly in the construction industry, modern project leaders are handling a much greater diversity of tasks in different types of organizations in every sector of the economy. These 'new-style' projects may have similarities to traditional construction or engineering projects, where there are hard criteria of time, cost and specification to be met. Just as often, however, their goals are most ambiguous, and project leaders have to contend much more with organizational politics, external environmental or marketing pressures and, above all, the needs of individuals inside and outside the organization to have an influence on the project. These factors have a fundamental effect on the project leader's role.

Traditional projects have often been depicted as a triangle (Figure 0.1).

In new-style projects the traditional triangle is set in a circle of additional factors (Figure 0.2) which have always existed but which have become more important as the project approach has spread across the whole spectrum of business and organizational activity.

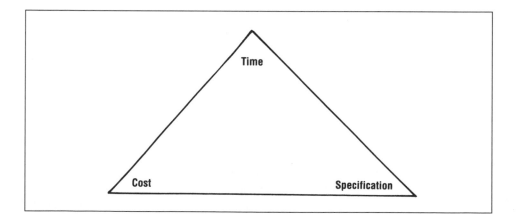

Figure 0.1 The project triangle

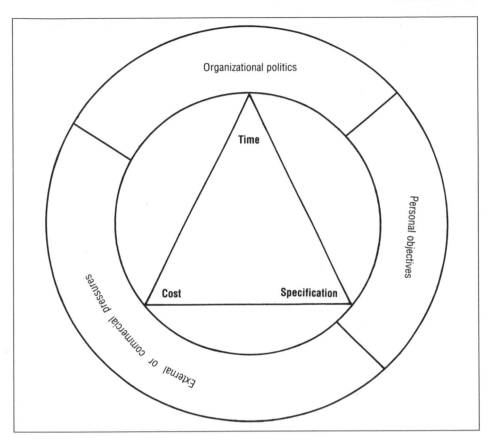

Figure 0.2 The triangle in context

The centre of gravity of any project is always somewhere within the triangle, whilst the size and position of the segments in the outer circle are different for every project.

Types of projects now being undertaken

New-style projects, like traditional ones, vary in scale, duration and complexity. They range from installing new computer systems to introducing new appraisal systems, from organizing an office move to launching a new product, from researching and testing a new drug to making a bid for a major new advertising account, from implementing a new management information system to managing the take-over and integration of another company. Whether in manufacturing, retail, financial services, local government, the health service or a charitable organization, there is usually one person, the project leader, whose role it is to ensure the project is completed successfully. There has been a huge growth

5

recently in the number of people performing this role. Most of them are technical specialists. Many come from line jobs and are totally unprepared for a role that demands such different and complex skills. Many of them fail. John Kingsley, with his construction project management experience, found that his new-style project leader role in the retail group required something else that he didn't seem to have.

This book is designed to help this growing number of project leaders to achieve greater success. It offers frameworks, and real examples, to help them develop a clear mental picture of what they are there to do. It provides checklists of core skills and tasks of successful project leadership. It will also assist senior managers in appointing project leaders; it will enable them to appreciate the difficult environment in which project leaders must operate, and to give the right kind of support. The project leader will be offered a wealth of practical tips about how to make projects successful.

Before discussing the details of the project leader's role, however, we will consider why organizations are using the project approach more and more, what 'new-style' projects are and how they differ from traditional construction or engineering projects. We will then look at the implications of these changes for project leadership in the organization.

Organizations in turmoil

Since the early 1960s, the limitations of the traditional hierarchical and functionally divided organization have been well documented. In particular, so-called 'bureaucratic' organizations find it difficult to be flexible and responsive in a dynamic and changing environment. They tend to inhibit innovation and individual initiative. The traditional divisions between professions and specialisms, and related restrictive practices add to the problems. The proliferation of sites both within a country and in different countries increases communication difficulties.

Organizations now exist in an environment even more turbulent than in the 1960s. The growing demands of international competition, increasingly sophisticated customers, an unprecedented complexity of new tasks, uncertainty in the environment, all require levels of performance, adaptability, flexibility and speed of innovation that, only a few years ago, would have seemed impossible. 'The best' is constantly being upgraded and redefined. In addition, better-educated employees are demanding more opportunities for involvement and development. The modern organization has to pay more attention to preserving people's motivation and commitment. All organizations are being forced to experiment with new ways of making things happen. The term 'networking organization' is increasingly being used to describe these more flexible, innovative and market-orientated organizations.

In recent years, new clues have begun to emerge about how these characteristics can be developed in large organizations, in spite of their in-built tendencies to bureaucracy and rigidity. Many are striving to create an infrastructure which promotes scale and financial weight, as well as the ability to change, adapt, respond and seize the initiative. Key words that run through these new experiments in organizations are 'involvement', 'innovation', 'complexity', 'commitment', 'creativity' and 'collaboration'. 'Organizational networking' brings all these together. It sets out to link different specialisms *horizontally* across the organization. It even extends outside to include suppliers, customers and joint ventures.

The theme of multi-disciplinary and multi-level teamworking appears repeatedly in studies of Japanese success. Their ability to create commitment through collaboration between managers and workers and between different specialists is the envy of the world. The future health of organizations depends on the ability to complement increasing specialization with successful integration of the separate specialisms to serve the wider goals. Only organizational networking can cross specialist boundaries and ensure shared understanding of the complex issues facing organizations. From this, commitment will grow, and success will follow.

Ask people to name the teams in their organization and you are likely to be given answers such as 'the sales team', 'the production team', 'the training department' and so on. These are functional teams defined by a formal structure. You may hear about the divisional team, the Board, or, in a project-based organization, certain project teams. These are cross-functional groupings, again defined by the formal organization structure.

There are, however, many other teams in an organization that most people don't 'see' in the same way. To recognize these 'invisible' teams, we must think a bit more about the nature of teamworking in modern organizations.

What is organizational networking?

Organizational networking is the sum of individual and organizational activity actively directed towards collaborative effort between individuals and groups both inside and outside the organization.

Organizational networking is therefore the *total* set of processes whereby individuals from different parts of the organization, and outside it, work in an active collaborative way to achieve a shared task or objective. It is the antithesis of people working independently, purely within set boundaries, waiting for others to approach them, or taking up adversarial positions in relation to others. A minimum amount of collaborative activity has to take place between individuals in totally different parts and levels of an organization to make it work at all. Experience and research suggest that increasing the range, scope and volume of collaboration between individuals at different levels, across different functions and across organizational boundaries is a great advantage.

Many organizations are now creating more flexible temporary structures to complement the formal ones. Whilst the traditional structures require teamworking to manage ongoing processes, the temporary task structures (all of which are really projects) are being created to respond to change, to provide flexibility and to stimulate innovation and productivity. The British Council has set up a new division to bring together consortia to bid for and subsequently manage large educational contracts overseas; a number of specialists, previously working completely independently in their own fields, combine their expertise for each project. This is an example of competitive and environmental pressures forcing organizations to become more fluid and responsive, yet simultaneously more tightly knit, in order to bring multi-disciplinary, multi-functional skills to bear on increasingly complex and fast-changing problems. Specialists are required to step across into each other's territories and enjoy a dynamic and robust interaction hardly possible in a more traditional structure.

Another feature of these projects is that they form, dissolve and re-form, bringing together people because of what they can contribute, not because of who they are. Organizational networking is about removing boundaries and barriers, creating a web of links and contacts between individuals so as to get things done.

The production director of a high-turnover knitwear factory where the mix was always changing according to fashion and season, defined his problem:

> There are four people who should be the key to the launch of our new range. The trouble is that the organization chart makes them look more like the four legs of a table. The structure doesn't say that they are a project team but they have to be. There's the marketing manager, the production planner, the designer and the distribution manager. One cannot sneeze without the others being affected. And if they don't get it right, and can't see themselves as a project team, then I know only too well what that does to my cash flow if the range doesn't go on sale at the right time.

Each of the four people here had to be very different, but each needed a teamworking mentality. They were so much more powerful when they saw themselves as a project team.

There are many individuals, whose roles are not related in the formal organization structure, who have to work collaboratively to achieve something. They must be seen to be in every way as much of a team as the formal teams defined by the structure. The project leader's role is to link together people who have a contribution to make to solving a problem or bringing about a change.

Virtual teams with real tasks

Many large organizations use project teams to stimulate this collaboration and commitment across the organization. Smaller organizations, as they grow, are also working hard in the same direction. Organizational teams (frequently temporary in nature) are being created to bring together individuals from the different specialisms. These teams may be called 'project groups', 'task forces', 'networks', 'quality teams' or 'virtual teams', but their aim is the same. Significant authority and responsibility are devolved to them to create and implement solutions within a broad framework of support provided by the organization. A great deal of work goes into helping previously unconnected individuals develop a sense of common purpose. Involvement in these teams releases untapped talent, enthusiasm and commitment in the organization. Teams are deliberately created to stimulate communication and cross-fertilization in order to produce better-quality solutions to complex problems.

The projects we are considering here are dynamic means of change. They require the skills and knowledge of a whole range of people, sometimes on a regular or permanent basis, sometimes on an occasional basis. A project team is often a frequently fluctuating body of people from different levels of the organization, many of whom may never meet each other. As indicated earlier, the term 'organizational networking' describes this type of collaboration. It has a number of characteristics distinguishing it from the more traditional teamworking:

- The people in the team are spread throughout the organization, and frequently outside it as well.
- Team members seldom work full-time on the project, and often have other priorities and departmental loyalties which compete for their attention.
- Team members are often not under the direct organizational control of the project leader, and may even be higher in the hierarchy than the project leader.
- Being scattered and lacking visible coherence, the team members may not think of themselves, nor be seen by the organization, as parts of a project team.

The team can be defined as: 'All those individuals who have a significant contribution to make to the successful achievement of the project through one or more of these factors:

- their technical or specialist expertise
- their sponsorship, political support or commitment
- their expectations of and interest in its outcome.'

Creating a sense of being a team in previously unconnected specialists with other priorities is a complex skill. Project leaders have to build a committed project group, often against all the odds, and then achieve the full benefits, both personally and to the organization, of this form of cross-functional collaboration.

We believe that the traditional views of project management must be adjusted to deal with the new reality. A new style of project management is required.

A new definition of project management

We would define this new style project management as *'managing the visible and invisible team to achieve the objectives of the stakeholders'*.

Six concepts underlie this definition. The first four are explicit:

- *The visible team* – the group of people working directly on the project who come together from time to time to make the project happen. Very often they, and the project leader, are working only part-time on the project. To complicate matters, the project leader frequently starts off with no people allocated to the project, and may need to gather a visible team by informal processes. Sometimes members of the visible team come from outside the leader's own organization.
- *The invisible team* – the group of people who contribute indirectly to the work of the visible team; their co-operation and support are vital to the success of the project. As with the visible team they may be inside or outside the organization. Project leaders neglect the management and motivation of this network at their peril.
- *The multiple stakeholders* – the people who have an interest in the outcome of the project. There are always a variety of stakeholders in any project, but Figure 0.3 illustrates those who are normally involved. (Sometimes these stakeholders may be combined, as shown, but this depends upon the nature of the particular project.)

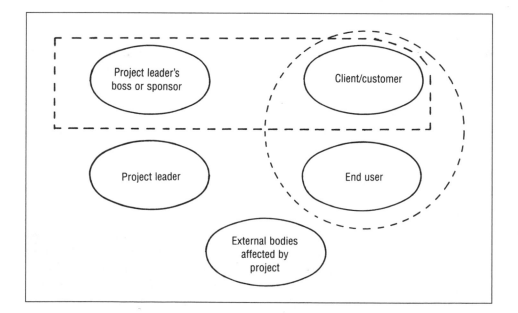

Figure 0.3 Stakeholders in a project

- *Managing organizational networking* – project leaders consciously directing the efforts of all involved inside and outside the organization towards collaboration of high quality. Teamworking spreads beyond traditional boundaries. Networking largely supersedes hierarchy. Co-operation and mutual enabling replace adversarial and controlling relationships.

The remaining two concepts are implicit:

- *The organizational context* – all projects are established to achieve a task, usually within clear constraints of time and cost. What makes new style projects more complex is the greater impact of organizational factors beyond the immediate project. These are now central, not peripheral, to the project. There are numerous vested interests, often at odds with each other (as John Kingsley discovered). Every project concerns more than just time, cost and specification. It inevitably involves organizational politics, change (where some people gain and some lose) and the wider commercial, financial or strategic significance of the project to the organization as a whole. Project leaders who are just good at ensuring that the technical side of the task is done well often 'fail' because they lack sensitivity to the wider contextual factors represented by the circle in Figure 0.2. These factors require different skills. Technical skills alone are no longer enough to get you through.
- *The people factor* – as many fiascos are caused by inadequate people management as by insufficient skill in technical areas. This is evident from any analysis of disasters in traditional engineering and construction projects. Recent interviews with project leaders have confirmed the increasing importance of the people factor. It has always been there, but many good technical specialists have little experience or appetite for managing this essential dimension. Comments from the research included:
  - 'I need to look on myself as a manager rather than a technician.'
  - 'One of the problems I have is seeing people unhappy and not knowing why they are unhappy.'
  - 'I constantly have to cope with people who "know better".'
  - 'I always have to judge which works better in a particular circumstance – playing Mr Nice Guy or being a real ogre!'

The concepts in action

If we refer back to the problems of John Kingsley and Liz Jones we can see how an appreciation of these concepts would help them to lead their project teams more effectively.

John had both a visible and invisible team, with team members coming from both within and outside the organization; there were multiple stakeholders, with differing expectations, and from different levels in the organization. Above all, his biggest single problem was the human factor – 'They make it so complicated here, everyone wants their say.'

Liz's main problem was also how to manage conflicting interests to achieve the different objectives of the various stakeholders. The teamworking skills required to motivate a replacement team, often working apart from each other, were more important to her than an understanding of the technical aspects of the project. If she could motivate the team to perform better, and develop better relationships with the key stakeholders, then technical and financial support would be forthcoming.

Conclusion

This book aims to develop your understanding of these concepts. It introduces you to ways of improving your skills and of increasing your understanding. Thus you will become a more effective project leader. You will be better able to operate in the exciting new field of project management which is crucial in developing modern organizations. You will be better able to manage both the visible and invisible team, with internal and external members, to be aware of all the stakeholders and meet their needs. Whilst technical knowledge can never be neglected, it is the people skills which are the key to successful project management.

Part I
The project leader

In this section we focus on the skills and competence needed by the modern project leader and in particular how these skills need to be employed differently in different types of 'open', 'temporary' and 'closed' projects. The section provides both an overview and a foundation of core ideas which will be developed further in later sections.

1 What makes a good project leader?

A project leader responsible for a team developing a new drug attended a recent course in project management because, he said, he thought his 'job was impossible' and he hoped 'that the course would provide him with the Holy Grail of project management'. By the end of the programme he accepted that there were no absolute answers, but there were guidelines or concepts which could make his job less impossible.

What are the main features of project leadership, and how do they differ from those involved in being a line manager or specialist?

The role of the project leader

All the project leaders we have met think that, because their projects are unique, their roles must also be unique. However, analysis shows that there are common characteristics in every project leader's role, not necessarily found in other managerial roles.

Outside line hierarchy

A project is specific and often outside 'day-to-day' business. It is therefore outside the normal line hierarchy. It may even go beyond a matrix of responsibility and authority. There are unusual and temporary links to senior managers. There are few formal or informal codes of practice on how a project leader should respond upwards and downwards.

Many project leaders find they have to establish their own lines of contact. They have to determine their own definitions of success. They have to make their own demands for resources and means to monitor performance. Outside the 'normal' hierarchy they have some freedom to determine their own destiny, just because they are out of the ordinary. On the other hand, they may meet considerable opposition to their demands and initiatives because they are seen by colleagues to be rocking the boat or undermining the status quo.

15

More than specialists

Even very senior specialists in organizations, such as company lawyers or personnel directors, rarely have direct personal responsibility for a line activity important to the company. To be effective such specialist managers have to build strong channels of informal influence. These are based on their personal credibility and their ability to ensure that their expertise has an impact on the overall business. Giving correct advice is often not sufficient. They have to persuade line managers of its application and direct benefits. For example, management accountants spend much of their time interpreting financial data on behalf of line managers and presenting it in a comprehensible way. Rarely can they insist that a line manager listens to them if, in the end, he/she decides that the information is wrong or insignificant. The specialist doesn't usually carry the ultimate responsibility. The project leader, however, *is* responsible for the success or failure of the project. This makes it easier to insist on the provision of resources, but it also means having to deal with the numerous and often conflicting interests which are at play. The project leader has to be as persuasive and influential as a specialist colleague.

The characteristics of a project leader's role

A project leader is:

- responsible for the achievement of project goals which are limited but require very visible and dynamic activity. In relation to the project, the role is similar to that of a general manager.
- unable to hide. It is clearly apparent who is in charge. It is therefore a high risk role.
- limited in direct authority. This varies according to the project leader's position, but it is usually necessary to negotiate for resources and support from a wide network of people inside and outside the organization.
- expected to cut across normal organizational boundaries and customs and needs to be unconventional in approach. Dealing with resistance or opposition is very demanding.
- often working in areas new for the company – new technology, new markets or new approaches to old situations. The unknown and unpredictable are often feared by many in the mainstream organization. Credibility may be low to start with, and needs to be built up.

The project leader's direction finder – The Six Lookings

Figure 1.1 illustrates the idea that a project leader must look in six directions: upwards, outwards, forwards, backwards, downwards and inwards:

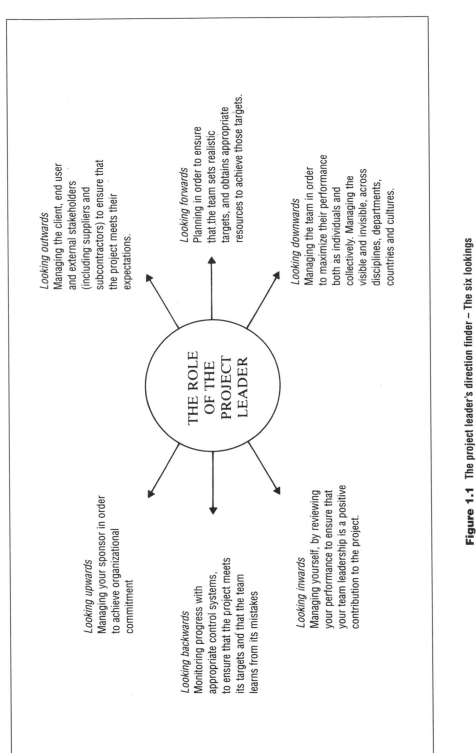

Looking outwards
Managing the client, end user and external stakeholders (including suppliers and subcontractors) to ensure that the project meets their expectations.

Looking forwards
Planning in order to ensure that the team sets realistic targets, and obtains appropriate resources to achieve those targets.

Looking downwards
Managing the team in order to maximize their performance both as individuals and collectively. Managing the visible and invisible, across disciplines, departments, countries and cultures.

Looking upwards
Managing your sponsor in order to achieve organizational commitment

Looking backwards
Monitoring progress with appropriate control systems, to ensure that the project meets its targets and that the team learns from its mistakes

Looking inwards
Managing yourself, by reviewing your performance to ensure that your team leadership is a positive contribution to the project.

THE ROLE OF THE PROJECT LEADER

Figure 1.1 The project leader's direction finder – The six lookings

- *Looking upwards* – The person who initiates the project – the project leader's boss – is the sponsor of the project. The sponsor provides an organizational umbrella. The sponsor is also, of course, an individual with personal reasons for asking you to do the job in question. It is important to know these reasons. For example, unless you know why the organization wishes to install a new computerized management information system, you may tread on a number of sensitive toes and find it impossible to complete the project successfully. So looking upwards and managing your sponsor is an essential part of the project leader's role.
- *Looking outwards* – All projects have a client, an end user (who might be different from the client) and possibly a number of other external stakeholders (such as suppliers and subcontractors). Such parties have expectations of the project which you must seek to meet.

These first two facets of the project leader's role concern *managing the stakeholders*.

- *Looking backwards and looking forwards* – These two facets are part of the same function. As a project leader you will need appropriate control systems to ensure that you meet targets and learn from your mistakes. You cannot do this, however, without first looking forwards – establishing realistic plans, raising the necessary resources, and putting in place the appropriate monitoring and reporting systems.

These middle two facets of the project leader's role concern *managing the project life cycle*.

- *Looking downwards* – As the leader of a team, you have a responsibility to ensure that they perform well, both individually and collectively. One theme of this book is how you can do this in the context of your organization.
- *Looking inwards* – It is all too easy to become too involved in the day-to-day tasks of a project and forget that your own performance has a big impact on the overall progress of the project.

These last two facets of the project leader's role concern *managing performance* – maximizing both your own performance and that of your team.

There are, then, three dimensions to a project leader's role:

- the management of *stakeholders*
- the management of the *project life cycle*
- the management of *performance*.

The project leader as integrator

You may now be coming to the conclusion that the variety and complexity of the project leader's role make it impossible! Many project leaders do feel that they would need to be super-human to do everything which is expected of them. How can any individual hope to hold on to all the complex threads of a modern project? The answer lies not in holding on, but in letting go! Let go of the assumption that you have to know everything and do everything yourself. Instead, see the leader's role as one which integrates, orchestrates, energizes and co-ordinates people and processes. The project leader should give as much emphasis to managing the organizational context as to managing the technical delivery.

Project leaders usually manage specialists in areas other than their own, who have to be brought together to produce effective results. So the project leader's own expertise may be important in commanding respect and credibility but be of limited use in actually ensuring that the job is done. A good example of this is the paediatrician who heads a child care unit in which his own abilities are combined with the specialisms of psychologists, physiotherapists, social workers and educationalists to provide a complete service to disadvantaged children.

So the project leader must be an integrator. Integration involves pulling together all the activities of the project, watching out for any links that are missing or broken. Integration must happen in all three dimensions of the stakeholder's project life cycle and team performance:

You may not feel you have the ability to act on different levels simultaneously, but it can certainly be developed with practice. One key is to recognize that you need others to help even if you don't have a formal project team. Another is to let go of your image of yourself as a particular technical specialist, and instead recognize that your new specialism is that of integrating your own and others' strengths and capabilities to the full.

In the words of one architect client of ours:

> I used to see my leadership role as being like rowing alone through treacle. If there were problems, I rowed harder and put more effort into the architecture. Now I realize that my role is actually to work on making the treacle thinner and on building up a team of different kinds of rowers with me as the cox! If I get the organizational context going with me and the teamworking right, the rest is easy!

This chapter deals with the core integrating processes that you, together with your team, will need in order to deal with the dynamic complexity of project leadership. We are not going to inundate you with lists of competencies or skills, but we will indicate what needs your attention and give you some practical ideas.

The integrative processes illustrated in Figure 1.2 are interrelated, so don't treat them in isolation. They apply across all three project leadership dimensions. Look at your target areas for renewed attention, revealed by the questionnaire at the end of this chapter, then follow through to the particular heading where the process is explained.

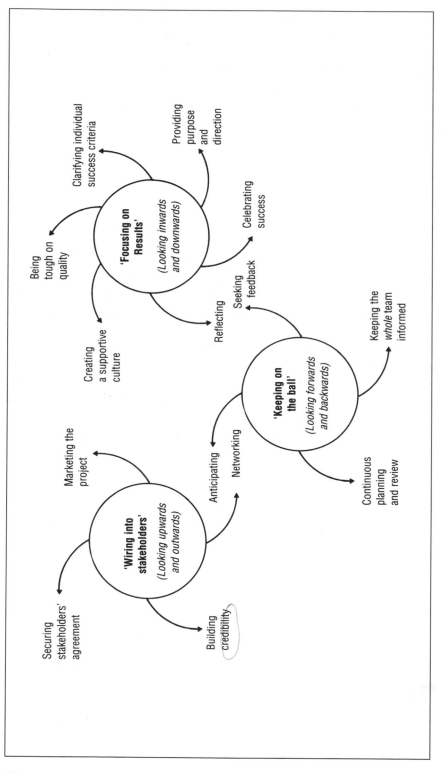

Figure 1.2 Fourteen integrative processes

'Wiring in' to stakeholders – Looking upwards and outwards

This is essential to building up strong, durable links with the important stakeholders. 'Wiring in' suggests making contact. The metaphor is intended to remind you that electrical wires are only useful if the current is flowing.

Securing stakeholders' agreement

New-style projects can have a bewildering number of stakeholders. You will soon come to realize that they all want something different! Establishing who the stakeholders are in your project and what they really want is never simple, even if it appears so. The first thing to do is to ask lots of questions. People are rarely clear in their first pronouncements and you can build your credibility very rapidly by helping them to clarify their ideas. You can also point out where their expectations clash with those of others and encourage the parties to talk to try to resolve areas of conflict. Gaining a real understanding of what they all want, and then getting agreement is a consummate skill in its own right. Reconciling the expectations of finance directors, design engineers, production people, marketing *and* the customer when developing a new product involves being a very skilled juggler! The skilled project leader often acts as a broker or negotiator to try to find a best-fit formula that meets as many needs as possible. Without this, you cannot succeed.

Building credibility

In creating a positive organizational context for your project, the single most useful (and most undervalued) resource you and your team can have is the positive support of your colleagues throughout the organization.

You have to earn this. You and your team members have to build your credits with the organization. Establish early on what leads your senior management to think that a project is well managed. Is it keeping within the budget? Is it overcoming technical difficulties? Is it being in tune with market or internal political movements? Show you appreciate the wider implications of your activity. If you know what they think is important and what makes them feel uncomfortable or suspicious about the health of a project, you and your team can set about demonstrating that you do appreciate their perspective. You will be worthy of their confidence and able to face difficult problems or push for what you need.

Building credits early on will stand you in good stead later in whatever project bargaining you need to undertake. You need to show that you understand:

- the technical impact – that you and your team appreciate the technical issues and difficulties which you (and they) face

- the financial impact – that you have thoroughly researched and analysed the financial costs, benefits and risks to which your project exposes the organization
- the people impact – that you understand that the outcomes of organizational projects frequently mean changes for many people in the organization, some positive, some negative; you need to manage the project to gain widespread commitment and satisfaction, whilst minimizing negative, de-motivating or destructive consequences.

At times, however, you may need to push very hard to secure something that's critical to your project and, in doing so, make yourself very unpopular in some quarters. As one personnel manager who was head of a group installing a new appraisal system said:

> That's when I really tested out whether the team had built up its credits in the organization. If we hadn't, there's no way we could have expected to get what we were demanding. We had to cash in a lot of credits that day, but the payoffs for the project were enormous. It was uncomfortable, but worth it.

Gaining access to resources against competitive challenges from other projects may be one of your headaches. Seldom is enough allocated to organizational projects. Raising resources and holding on to them is often a political problem in which the project's credibility rating is important. Whilst sometimes an organization will have a special budget for a project, further resources (especially people's time) often have to be obtained from various departments by negotiation and personal influence. Your project's reputation for being effective will help you in securing official and unofficial resources. If you are lacking in credits, your bargaining power will be weak.

Networking

Successful project leaders build networks of relationships to help them get things done. Spend time networking – talking to people informally to trade information and find out what is going on. Project leaders who are not plugged into the formal system of their organization and that of their clients often find themselves wrong-footed, surprised and left in an exposed position. Successful project leaders learn from what they hear and see. They learn that there are formal and informal ways of getting things done, of finding things out and of getting decisions made. They also use networking to test new ideas. Networking or 'asking around', is also an excellent way of spotting hidden talent that might benefit the project. It is said that by making no more than three telephone calls, The Skilled networker can access any information or specialist advice he/she may ever need!

Looking for ideas or information from a wide variety of sources can help you find ways of solving sticky problems or of tackling something that has not been done before in your organization.

Highly effective project teams also actively seek outside specialists to help them do things better. One project team studying acquisitions in France went and talked to another company in a totally different business which had recently taken over a French company. They picked up invaluable know-how which they could not have gained in any other way.

Marketing the project

A project is like a product. It needs to be well packaged and marketed if people are going to want to buy it. Remember – the merits of your project are not self-evident to everyone else. If they do not understand, value or support it, you have only your poor marketing to blame. So use all the simple marketing tools at your disposal, and find some invisible team members with the skills to help you make your project match the standards that are set for important products in your organization:

- Organize presentations (both formal and informal), particularly to explain why the whole project is important to the company, how it will be carried out and how people can help. Highlight the issues that will be of special interest to the audience – what's in it for them. Make it interesting, exciting and different.
- Plan and execute a marketing campaign throughout the project's life cycle to ensure it receives the attention and recognition it needs. A one-off activity in the start-up phase will be easily forgotten.
- Make sure that news of the project regularly reaches the eyes and ears of the influential. This can be achieved through formal reports, updates and newsletters. One project leader produced a regular, electronically published newsletter with the project logo on the cover. It was circulated widely and left in public areas such as the restaurant and reception.

Ensure that everyone who would *like* to know is kept in touch with your intentions and ideas, your progress and problems. Many project leaders deliberately plan for their team members to go out and talk about the project informally to pivotal people within the organization. We all know the informal rumour machine can send ideas around – you can use it to your advantage.

Keeping on the ball – Looking forwards and backwards

The project leader needs to think like a footballer in possession of the ball, constantly aware of the opposition's threats, of his own team's support and of the need to maintain the initiative.

Anticipating

We are continually surprised by the number of managers who *say* they're anticipating, but are in fact not looking beyond today's problems.

You need to be able to step back from the immediate pressures of the day, and look at the whole situation. Disasters rarely occur out of the blue; there are nearly always early warning signs if you look for them. Find short periods of time to run through any worrying situations, preferably with somebody else off whom you can bounce ideas. Just think through the implications, knock-on effects, contingencies. Ask yourself 'What is the worst scenario? How would I deal with that?'

A useful and well known way of looking at a project is the SWOT analysis:

Strengths	–	What's going in your favour?
Weaknesses	–	Where are you vulnerable?
Opportunities	–	What chances exist to take you forward?
Threats	–	What would knock you over?

Having carried out your own analysis, check it against your stakeholders' ideas.

One project leader described anticipating as 'getting myself and the team to play different videos of how the project might unfold and how we'd like it to unfold'.

Continuous planning and reviewing

We still find many project leaders who think that planning is something that needs to be done just once, at the beginning! This approach assumes that everything can be predicted in advance, which it never can. Continuous cycles of planning, doing and reviewing must take place throughout the project, and the greater the uncertainty and innovation, the more important this process is.

Two important tips for good planning are to know the limitations and benefits of one's tools, and to involve (and believe) those people who have the best-quality information. The tools must be manipulated by the project members and not vice versa. They must provide the information on which to make judgements and draw conclusions. Be wary of the 'wish-and-hope' type of information which is sometimes fed into sophisticated planning systems, only to distort the picture.

Planning and decision-making processes must not be allowed to degenerate into ritual. Their results must be made widely known and acted upon.

Review is the important next step after planning, and it must be constructive, not like these meetings described by a senior team manager in a torpedo development project:

> Our project review meetings are just nightmares. Everyone waits in silence for the project manager to pick them off one by one and tear them to shreds. It seems his main aim is to send us all off with our tails between our legs.

We all have a tendency when reviewing to point to the things that we did badly. The project leader must create a climate in which people face mistakes and poor performance honestly, but must not allow it to stop there. There is no point in identifying mistakes without learning from them and agreeing what will be done next time round.

Keeping the whole team informed

Are you keeping your sponsor up to date?

Successful project leaders do not become so absorbed in the fascinations of their own project as to believe that its merits are equally clear to everyone else. They recognize that, whilst their project is occupying all their time, the sponsor and the invisible team have many other demands being made upon them. It is an important task for project leaders to maintain interest and enthusiasm for the project. Even if it is very ably managed, with excellent technical performance, it can easily be rated low if those who make judgements are not kept well informed about what is happening. A regular dialogue with senior managers should ensure that they are never taken by surprise.

Invisible team members are frequently either forgotten or taken for granted. Project leaders tend to assume that they will be there when needed, forgetting that they have other priorities and deadlines to meet besides those of the project. It's important, therefore, to involve them early and prepare the ground so that they know what will be required of them and when. They need managing just like any other team members.

Secretaries are often much neglected and under-utilized invisible team members. One secretary commented:

> They never even *told* me before this that I'd have to be the project's secretary – they just sort of assumed I would, that I had nothing else to do! Even now, I have to keep bullying them to remember that I do have a real role in the project and that I need to know the decisions and plans that they hatch up. They'd forget me otherwise!

As new stakeholders and team members become involved, you need to put a lot of effort into introducing them to the project and explaining what is going on. This takes time and requires remembering that they are starting at first base.

Seeking feedback

> Tell us how we're doing. We want both the good news – to reassure us and make us feel good – and the bad news – so that we can do something about it quickly.

This request was made by one project team to its principal stakeholders. Asking for feedback is so much more effective than waiting for it. It provides invaluable early warnings of any problems. The request itself, and any necessary follow-up action, build a project team's credits within the organization. You don't need to have anything as structured as a questionnaire – there are several other ways, such as review meetings and informal conversations.

Of course, it's no good asking for feedback and then ignoring it when it comes. We know of a case in which clients were asked how they saw the company. The answer came back: 'You are arrogant.' The company's response was: 'Yes we know; that's what they said last time we asked!'

Focusing on results – Looking inwards and downwards

It's up to you, as project leader, to maintain motivation, momentum and direction.

Providing purpose and direction

You can help create a sense of purpose amongst your team in a number of ways. The first is to help their understanding to go beyond the project specification to the underlying reasons *why* the project is important to the organization as a whole. We worked with a project team developing a major new piece of software in a financial service company. The technical specification was clear and the project complex, but somehow the systems analysts and programmers involved weren't fired up about it – there were other more technically interesting projects around. The turning point came when the team spent an hour with the Chief Executive and the Marketing Director, who explained how the new system was a crucial part of the company's aggressive expansion strategy, designed to give it a competitive edge in customer service. This appreciation of the project's wider purpose triggered a new and real sense of motivation in the team. It also unleashed a wealth of new ideas about how the system could be significantly improved and finished more quickly than the existing plan proposed.

The second way of creating purpose is to tease out of the team how the project could be used to achieve some of their own personal visions and aspirations. It is surprising how often people see that being in a good project team can enable them to achieve ambitions they could not realize on their own. In the same software team, a team decision to use an innovative new programming language gave each member an opportunity for rapid self-development. It also created excitement by taking the risk of going for a much more ambitious solution with significant payoffs for the organization.

The third way to create purpose and direction lies in the way you, the project leader, communicate your own excitement, conviction and sense of mission about the project. If *you* are not very enthusiastic about it, it's very difficult to expect others to be motivated. Demonstrate your desire to sustain purpose, direction and momentum by communicating conviction, a sense of urgency and a constant search for better or quicker ways of doing things.

Clarifying individual success criteria

The project as a whole must have clear objectives, defined in terms of time and cost. But these must be translated into clear work goals agreed with each individual, specifying what work will be done, by when and within what constraints. Always make sure that the different jobs are co-ordinated with each other.

Particularly in projects with high levels of uncertainty, team members are given considerable scope in terms of how they reach their objectives, but you need to demonstrate through your attitudes and behaviour what is acceptable and what is not. How people discharge their responsibilities will directly affect the success of the project. A salesperson who – anxious to promote the virtues of the project to the client – 'bends' the truth creates unreasonable expectations and discredits the project. The culture of the organization itself is important here. For example, pushiness and aggressive persistence are sometimes seen as virtues, whereas in other companies more subtle (or devious!) ways of behaving are required.

Being tough on quality

Having set individual success criteria, you have to follow up to ensure that they are met. Effective project leaders discipline themselves to be tough on quality, and they encourage the same attitude in others. They set high standards for themselves and their team, and they ensure that any lapses are checked immediately.

Television current affairs programmes, for example, often make last-minute changes to the graphics they use. The graphics person works to achieve the high standards set by the team, despite the personal inconvenience of redoing work. The project leader insists that this happens when it needs to, and that team members know why. Anything that's not good enough is not accepted. When an individual is underperforming, the project leader has to address the situation speedily, explaining why the performance is unacceptable, and helping the person to improve.

Creating a supportive culture

To maintain high performance in the team, you need to give support in every way possible. You might simply ask people how you could help them to do their job more quickly or easily. Or you might effect introductions to other parts of the organization when an individual team member feels inhibited. Perhaps you can provide some extra resource on a temporary basis to help a team member under pressure. You might be able to relieve a bottleneck and stop people feeling that they are carrying an unfair burden.

It's very important that interest in the quality of results is shared across technical boundaries. Team members should be able to challenge and support colleagues in the interest of achieving a better result. There should be plenty of frank discussion, full of constructive criticism, with everybody concentrating on the issues and not on the shortcomings of particular individuals. It should be the aim of the project leader to create an atmosphere in which self-criticism rather than criticism of others is the rule, and in which people are free to say what they feel, and be listened to.

Reflecting

Introspection, self-analysis and quiet reflection do not come naturally to people of action. They want to get on and *do* things. One chief executive we know admitted as much, but remarked how frequently his business problems came into perspective when he was shaving! Many others we know have said that they take stock best when walking the dog; others have sudden flashes of inspiration and clarity in moments of wakefulness during the night.

Research into effective learning confirms the importance of the natural process of reflection, and pulling back from day-to-day concerns to see them in perspective. Researchers at Shell have called this the 'helicopter quality'. They found it to be the best single predictor of suitability for senior management. We are convinced that the same goes for effective project leaders. They consciously build in time to reflect, to survey the whole picture and, above all, to review their own performance. It is appropriate sometimes to do this with a colleague, team member or consultant, to provide the necessary mixture of challenge and support, monitoring your own stress levels and discovering what you find difficult to handle and why. A stressed project leader usually passes the stress on to others.

Celebrating success

Effective project teams and leaders help themselves to maintain momentum by celebrating their collective and individual achievements and successes along the way. Interim targets are important markers of success. Project leaders are always looking for ways of recognizing and celebrating achievements and contributions. Simple ways in which you can do this include:

- sending a personal handwritten note offering congratulations and thanks
- talking or writing publicly about team members who are outstanding, describing what they have done and why they were so successful
- holding an impromptu party or get-together to celebrate success
- saying 'well done' and 'thank you' spontaneously.

Team members will respond in different ways. Experience and observation will help you discover the best approach in each case.

When commenting on the results produced by a team member, outstanding project leaders often say: 'It takes a very special sort of person to do this work.' They are modest about their own contribution, making sure it is not more highly valued than that of other team members. Respect for the capabilities and efforts of others in the visible and invisible team is a common characteristic of individuals whose teams produce fine results.

Project leaders' competencies

Recently, we were asked by a retail chain to help them decide what the core competencies of project leaders are. So we asked project leaders themselves, their sponsors and team members what makes the difference, in their experience, between an average or poor project leader and those who do well. They told us that these competencies make the difference:

- The ability to explain complicated things simply and in understandable language.
- Don't panic and become hyperactive or alternatively become paralysed into inactivity – stay calm and find a step-by-step way forward with the team.
- Face up to problems, find out the causes and make proposals to management and customers.
- Let people know what's happening all the time – team members, senior managers and customers – don't default into mushroom management, because everybody expects the worst. Knowing the good and the bad news are equally important.
- The 'matrix mind', keeping an eye on the vision or the big picture, whilst having a finger on the pulse of the project's progress.

Interestingly these competencies assume technical abilities, but do not see technical superiority as making *the difference*. Being able to interact and communicate while managing the project's tasks seems to be the key.

Conclusion

Only you can judge what proportion of your time you should allocate to each part of the integrating process. But as the project progresses, you should be asking whether any adjustments are called for. Many project leaders are too reactive – they revel in firefighting and crisis management, instead of balancing these skills with the more productive, strategic approach. One thing is clear – you should always create small but significant periods of reflection time. Without this you will never even realize if your priorities are upside down.

Create some reflection time now by completing the following questionnaire, which will highlight your strengths and weaknesses in 'The Six Lookings'.

Questionnaire

To what extent are each of these statements true of you and your team? Try to make your judgement honestly and put a cross at what you consider is the appropriate point on the scale.

	Not at all true	*Very true*

A

1. I can confidently say that I keep fully informed everyone who wants to be. — 1- -2- -3- -4- -5
2. My team is good at making invisible team members feel they belong. — 1- -2- -3- -4- -5
3. Both I and all members of the team are very clear about our targets. — 1- -2- -3- -4- -5
4. I have ensured that my project has appropriate mechanisms for measuring progress. — 1- -2- -3- -4- -5
5. My team members would say that I provide them with a lot of support to enable them to do their jobs better. — 1- -2- -3- -4- -5
6. I have clearly demonstrated to my senior management that I understand the full impact of my project on the organization. — 1- -2- -3- -4- -5

B

1. I know how to get things done informally in the organization. — 1- -2- -3- -4- -5
2. I am honest with myself. — 1- -2- -3- -4- -5
3. I am not caught out by not having enough resources when I need them. — 1- -2- -3- -4- -5
4. I feel fine asking my sponsor for help. — 1- -2- -3- -4- -5
5. I review individual performance and progress with team members regularly. — 1- -2- -3- -4- -5
6. We are good at keeping everyone informed honestly about our progress. — 1- -2- -3- -4- -5

		Not at all true				*Very true*

C

1. My team genuinely regard essential people outside the organization as part of our team.   1- -2- -3- -4- -5
2. I take active steps to manage my stress.   1- -2- -3- -4- -5
3. Team members share with me the responsibility for planning and anticipating.   1- -2- -3- -4- -5
4. When things go wrong, we are good at taking effective action to put things right quickly.   1- -2- -3- -4- -5
5. I help my sponsor to help me by keeping him/her fully informed.   1- -2- -3- -4- -5
6. I put time and effort into developing our effectiveness in working as a team.   1- -2- -3- -4- -5

D

1. I am constantly trying to anticipate the problems that lie over the horizon.   1- -2- -3- -4- -5
2. I communicate conviction and confidence about the project to others.   1- -2- -3- -4- -5
3. We have a clearly-developed strategy for marketing the project within the organization.   1- -2- -3- -4- -5
4. All my team are fully aware of the project's importance to the organization.   1- -2- -3- -4- -5
5. I fully understand the expectations of all my project's stakeholders.   1- -2- -3- -4- -5
6. My project team never repeats the same mistake.   1- -2- -3- -4- -5

E

1. Much of my information for planning comes from members of the team or even outsiders.   1- -2- -3- -4- -5
2. I make conscious decisions about changing my priorities at each stage of the project life cycle.   1- -2- -3- -4- -5
3. I understand the politics at the top of my organization.   1- -2- -3- -4- -5
4. Team members share with me the responsibility for managing important external relationships.   1- -2- -3- -4- -5
5. I am aware of the personal strengths and weaknesses of my team members.   1- -2- -3- -4- -5
6. Team members share with me the responsibility for keeping things on track.   1- -2- -3- -4- -5

F

1. I am seldom caught out by unforeseen events.   1- -2- -3- -4- -5

	Not at all true	*Very true*

2. I seek regular feedback from others about how to improve my performance as project leader. 1- -2- -3- -4- -5

3. I am successful at persuading other departments to give me the resources I need. 1- -2- -3- -4- -5

4. I bring members of the team together regularly. 1- -2- -3- -4- -5

5. I feel confident in confronting and trying to resolve disagreements at a senior level that affect my project. 1- -2- -3- -4- -5

6. There's always a good feeling throughout the team when we pass an important landmark in the project. 1- -2- -3- -4- -5

G

1. I take time out to think about how effectively I am leading the project. 1- -2- -3- -4- -5

2. I can always have access to senior management when I need it. 1- -2- -3- -4- -5

3. I am good at imagining what might happen in the future. 1- -2- -3- -4- -5

4. We have reliable sources of feedback about how we're doing. 1- -2- -3- -4- -5

5. My project's team members are clear about the performance I expect of them. 1- -2- -3- -4- -5

6. I have all the contacts I need both inside and outside the organization. 1- -2- -3- -4- -5

On the following table, mark in opposite the relevant statement your score on the 1–5 scale – that is if you scored yourself as 4 on Statement A6 then record 4 against A6 below, and so on. Then add up your score for each element. You are best at managing the element with the highest score, and need to work at improving your management of the element with the lowest score.

LOOKING UPWARDS

	Score
A 6.	____
B 4.	____
C 5.	____
D 5.	____
E 3.	____
F 5.	____
G 2.	____
TOTAL	____

LOOKING OUTWARDS

	Score
A 2.	____
B 1.	____
C 1.	____
D 3.	____
E 4.	____
F 3.	____
G 6.	____
TOTAL	____

LOOKING BACKWARDS

	Score
A 4.	_____
B 6.	_____
C 4.	_____
D 6.	_____
E 6.	_____
F 6.	_____
G 4.	_____
TOTAL	_____

LOOKING FORWARDS

	Score
A 3.	_____
B 3.	_____
C 3.	_____
D 1.	_____
E 1.	_____
F 1.	_____
G 3.	_____
TOTAL	_____

LOOKING DOWNWARDS

	Score
A 5.	_____
B 5.	_____
C 6.	_____
D 4.	_____
E 5.	_____
F 4.	_____
G 5.	_____
TOTAL	_____

LOOKING INWARDS

	Score
A 1.	_____
B 2.	_____
C 2.	_____
D 2.	_____
E 2.	_____
F 2.	_____
G 1.	_____
TOTAL	_____

2 The project in the organization

If you think of the conversations you hear, you might conclude that the word 'project' is applied to a number of different activities. There are projects to move to Milton Keynes, to develop a new airline booking system, to re-engineer the purchasing process, to change the organizations's culture, to develop computer technicians' competencies and to joint venture with a business partner to deliver a new service.

Can all these diverse activities be managed with the same project management methods? Do all project leaders need a comprehensive skill range, or are some much better suited to some projects than others? Are there project features that identify what sort of project needs to be managed in which way?

The continuum of project types

In broad terms we find it helpful to describe three different project types along a continuum (Figure 2.1). We call these 'concrete', 'occasional' and 'open' – of course, in practice, various projects will fall in between, combining the characteristics. Sometimes projects which start as 'open' or 'occasional' become 'concrete' as they progress.

The three project types are distinguished from each other by three criteria:

- *The extent to which output can be defined*
  - *Highly specific projects* have, at the beginning, precise, clear concrete outputs or deliverables. *Concrete* projects are clear at the start what the deliverables should be.
  - *Low-specificity projects* are not clear in the early stages about what outputs are to be obtained. They are *open*. There are many possibilities that need to be investigated. The main aim is to clarify the potential outputs systematically and choose which is most relevant.
- *The level of structure and formality* – the extent to which there is clear definition of roles, a hierarchy of teams or sub-projects.

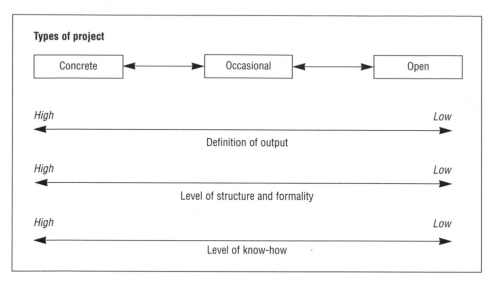

Figure 2.1 Project type continuum

- Do formal planning tools and procedures exist to co-ordinate and monitor activities and budgets?
- *Concrete projects* often have clear roles, systems and procedures consistent with those used elsewhere in the organization.
- *Occasional projects* used as vehicles for organizational change or to tackle one-off actions do not have 'ready-to-hand' structures and procedures. These projects have to build their own. Often the leader and team members have other line management jobs as well.
- *Open projects* may not see the need for any roles or systems. They rely upon the energy and interest of the project team to organize themselves as required and are very informal.

- *The level of know-how* – what know-how is available in the project team and the wider organization? In practice this means: how used are 'we' to dealing with these kinds of problems, or technical questions? In some projects there may be very tough issues that have to be solved, but if similar situations have been successfully managed previously, there is confidence that previous experience and expertise will win through.
  - These kinds of projects tend to be *concrete*, the existing know-how, both technical and 'street-wise', in terms of how to do things, will be high. There will be some ambiguity and new things to be learnt, but probably not in many critical areas at the same time.
  - *Occasional* projects are more frequently troubled by the range of ambiguous aspects. Inexperience, in terms of technical issues and how to do things, is high. These projects are often internal to the organization, and may be cutting new paths across the company culture as well as

trying to accomplish something new. Existing know-how may be limiting, or even unhelpful, holding back changes.

- When the project is *open*, experimentation is the order of the day. Innovations are often spawned in this way by finding out what is possible and how to do it. Little is known inside the organization, and sometimes outside it, so much has to be learnt through a planned process of trial and review when past experience is unlikely to help.

It is important to understand the project continuum because different types of project require very different leadership strategies and skills.

Concrete projects

Concrete projects (Figure 2.2) will be easily recognized by companies in the construction and aerospace industries. Other familiar examples are office moves or facilities installations, systems development (especially centralized systems), logistics, exhibition organizing, theatrical/film production and new product launches.

In all these examples, for many years projects have been an effective way of organizing work. Each job will be significantly different in content, but well-tried methods have been developed for tendering, writing specifications, estimating, planning and controlling. The skills and specialist know-how needed are clear, the particular constellation will be different, but everybody can easily identify what will be required. Formal, documented procedures – sometimes computerized – exist, and there is historical experience of what goes wrong and how long tasks take. People will be used to working in project teams and will rapidly fit into a new project.

A company that builds and commissions packing facilities world-wide has a clearly-defined project structure, with project leaders and senior project leaders. Project leaders would lead a project concerned with replacing production equipment in an existing plant, whilst senior project leaders would be responsible for the designing, building and commissioning of a plant in a distant and, to the company, unfamiliar part of the world. In this company there is a broad understanding of how to run a business using well-defined project teams with engineering technology that, whilst always incorporating advances, is well understood.

Another illustration of a concrete project is the naval base refitment team responsible for overhauling and refurbishing all classes of naval vessels within tight time schedules and even tighter budgets. They use many specialist subcontractors and combine civilian and naval staff. Estimating techniques are based on solid historical practice. The specialists needed are determined by tried and tested systems.

37

Characteristics

- Full-time leader
- Full-time visible team members – with clear roles, specialisms and hierarchy
- Project owner and sponsor are named and active
- Resources allocated and formal decision-making
- Project team and organization very experienced in this sort of project – know what to expect
- Well-established systems for estimating, planning and controlling.

Advantages

High levels of relevant experience

Accepted	Individuals and organizations are comfortable with concrete projects. Well-understood relationships, structures and risks
Controlled	Methods and tools tried and tested.

Disadvantages

The cracks	Invisible team ignored. Play a relay race – passing the baton leads to mutual blaming
Adversarial	Potentially combative relationships with subcontractors or external agents
Systems dominate	Become rituals with a life of their own, leading to surprises and persistent unaddressed problems consuming unproductive time
Critical gap	Client's and sponsor's needs become remote and hazy
Myopia	Technical dominance of one discipline closes out other considerations.

Figure 2.2 Concrete projects

Occasional projects

As we move across the project type continuum, the projects become less formal, less durable, less familiar and less established within the organization than the concrete type. Frequently they are internally-focused vehicles to achieve change in the way things are done, combining people from across organizational, geographical or professional boundaries who do not normally work together (Figure 2.3). Examples drawn from a wide range are:

- designing a new industrial relations negotiating structure
- introducing total quality or customer-focused initiatives
- defining and implementing a new product development process
- introducing robots on the shop floor
- creating a new strategic process
- defining how to enter a new market – perhaps in another culture.
- investigating a corporate policy for service standards.

Characteristics

- Often part-time leader
- Part-time team members with conflicting priorities of time and interest
- Unclear roles and relationships
- Cross-organizational or professional boundaries
- Unclear roles for sponsors and clients – what they want emerges
- Planning and control methods unfamiliar
- Resources a 'guesstimate'.

Advantages

Flexibility	Leader and team members nominated because of their interest. Leader has more choice of team members. Less precedents to restrict, and many innovative opportunities
	Chance to gain wider experience
Controlled	Internal projects cross normal organizational communication lines, break boundaries and gain the ear of senior people
	Have the sponsor's interest and positive attention, so a way for the leader to build credits.

Disadvantages

Priority conflicts	Project work competes with normal line activities, so is seen as rewarding and extra
Emerging direction	Frustration with the time and iterative discussions needed to clarify and agree options
	Pressure of ambiguity
Cultural resistance	Suspicion and awkwardness at working across unfamiliar boundaries. The 'not-invented-here' attitude of those left out of the project.

Figure 2.3 Occasional projects

Temporariness is the occasional project's main feature. The purpose, and therefore the deliverables, are less easily defined at the outset. A direction or theme will have been set, but the precise impact and benefits to the organization will not be specific.

Financial demands and effects are less tightly specifiable and may need to be planned and renegotiated in phases. Who should be involved may be unclear, and the commitment from team members and even the project leader is usually part-time. Often this particular activity has not been carried out by these people before, so they may not be confident in their abilities and will find it hard to anticipate problems. So much has to be learnt, individually and collectively about what the project entails, how to do it and how to work together. Planning will tend to be in short cycles of Plan–Do–Review–Re-plan (see Chapter 8), building rapidly on what has been learned in practice.

Simple planning tools will be all that is needed, and decision-making processes have to be defined and agreed by the project team and the sponsor.

Another example of a temporary project is the introduction of a new product into the competitive savoury biscuits market. Co-ordinating research, development, manufacturing, market testing, regulatory control and image presentation had been taking too long, so a temporary project was formed of all the participants who had a stake in progressing the product from research onto the shelf. This included people from outside the company, such as the advertising agency. Their brief was not only to define and develop the new product, but more importantly, to pioneer a radically different process for developing products that was much quicker.

Another occasional project is the task of developing a new strategic direction for a company. Here there may be many options; project teams may be asked to investigate, to examine, to pull together and finally to secure agreement to a preferred option. A company making simulators revised its after-sales service using a project team to identify what existed, what should exist, and therefore what the new service package might look like. This project was potentially huge. The team had to agree what to include and what to leave out and, perhaps more important, the basis for these decisions.

We have seen a considerable growth in occasional projects being used to define and implement organizational change. Taking people from across the depth and breadth of the organization means that problems can be understood from the many perspectives that exist, and widespread commitment can be generated to the solutions that are agreed. The solutions themselves are likely to be more easily implemented, and therefore more effective, because the implications of the problem are widely understood, options have been generated and people have been involved in the decision-making. Involving a large number of people early on generates more will and energy to make it happen.

Open projects

At the far end of the continuum are those projects whose objectives are unclear and where there is uncertainty about the direction or viability of what is being attempted (Figure 2.4).

An open project sounds like a non-project. Its objectives will often be fuzzy and may change frequently. There is accumulating evidence that small, unofficial projects (often called 'skunk works') produce significant innovations and are effective vehicles for change. Organizations which are concerned to harness rapidly the ideas and opportunities which present themselves at all levels encourage the use of informal projects – often just a small group of interested people gathered together by an enthusiastic individual. Their purpose is to test

Characteristics

- No formal leader. The most interested people will be the focal point
- Team members select themselves, attracted by the idea or opportunity
- Self-organizing activities and monitoring
- Try out low-key experiments until something works.

Advantages

Motivation	Individual spontaneity or energy can be harnessed without any strings
Creativity	Embryonic ideas have a chance to be tested, and enhanced into viable innovations or dropped
Low risk	Low resource investments, low visibility in the organization, so minimal consequences if it fails.

Disadvantages

Slow projects	Low priority, low resources, so remain good intentions that fade
Subversive	Low visibility can mean that success goes against mainstream activities and hijacks traditional wisdom. Friends need to be won at the right time.

Figure 2.4 Open projects

and develop new ideas for business improvement. The belief is that business improvements can be made not only by large schemes, carefully planned and handled by specialists, but also by pulling together and putting into practice a thousand small ideas. This type of project is more useful than may at first appear. An increasing number of companies are encouraging people to form spontaneous groups to resolve problems which they see as hindering their work.

Quality drives, customer-focused drives, innovation drives, performance improvement drives – all are promoting more open projects. For every open project that makes the grade and emerges with substantial results, there are many that fold or remain invisible.

Many open projects transform, as they become more formal, into either occasional or concrete projects. As they become more defined, with anticipatable benefits, they gain a sponsor, a more formal team and customer expectations. However, they have to put effort into building their 'market' or reason for existing in order to win internal support for the allocation of the resources necessary to grow. Examples are hard to trace because, if they are successful, they are well accepted. If they fail, nobody can remember them.

The main feature of open projects is that they enable limited experimentation because there is always limited time and even more limited resources. So open projects usually involve developing the first steps of embryonic innovations.

Examples are:

- research laboratories with small-scale experiments to investigate new substances
- developing new management development programmes

41

- applying more participative and empowering working practices.
- identifying applications for untried technology – e.g. electronic shopping.

The case of a software research engineer who developed new tools for optimizing the performance of a complex telecommunications network shows how small beginnings can become accepted. One person's interest was extended by very low-key experiments that subsequently developed into a sequence of small projects which, in turn, became a permanent unit whose job it was to continually improve the network's performance.

Open projects start small and invisible, but through their demonstrated success and the energy of the team involved in gaining support step-by-step, their potential impact becomes clear, and wider organizational commitment becomes mobilized.

Using the project continuum

Our experience tells us that there is a trend towards organizations developing a mixed portfolio of projects. This consists of a few big concrete projects and many occasional projects, plus a number of open projects. Sometimes this creates confusion because there are so many projects to manage, so the management of projects itself becomes an important task for senior managers. How to settle priorities, how to allocate and track resources and how to manage the project interface, not to mention duplications between projects? These are central questions that need to be resolved.

Amid this increasing confusion, the major purpose of the project continuum is to make sure, once you have decided in which type of project you are involved, that you have the appropriate structures and management expectations. We have witnessed considerable frustration between the project leader and the sponsor or project owner if they treat an occasional project as if it were concrete.

One example was a project set up to re-design the collective bargaining arrangements in an insurance company. Clearly, the deliverables were expected to be a new framework, organizational structures and procedures that would fit better with the flexible, flatter organization that was being introduced. So the project team kept analysing, investigating, consulting and putting together new frameworks. These would then be discussed with the project owner and were always found to be inadequate in some significant way. The project leader accused the sponsor of constantly moving the goal-posts. The sponsor began, as the weeks wore on, to question the technical capability (not to mention the intelligence) of the project leader.

The underlying problem was that they both thought the project was *concrete*, when in fact it was *occasional* and rather *open*! Although the general direction was easily understood, there were many options, with a complex array of advantages and disadvantages. Step-by-step iterative scoping (see Chapter 5) was needed to investigate the options and agree the overall success criteria of the new collective bargaining process. Only when this had been achieved could the options be narrowed down, agreed and then implemented.

Conversely, some organizations without a tradition of project management methods may put together a concrete project and try to run it like an occasional project. This leads to considerable confusion over who is doing what, and what the dependencies are. In fact, nobody is in control of the whole project, so there are some nasty surprises. The message is clear: if you know what type of project you are running, and consciously manage it as that type, you are much more likely to develop the appropriate structure and management processes. If there is incompatibility between the type of project, the way it is being structured and the expectation of key players, there will be severe difficulties in delivery.

Project leadership and the project continuum

The approach to a project is not the only consideration that is linked to the characteristics of a particular project: the demands on the project leader are also different. In Chapter 1, Figure 1.1 gave general guidelines for a project leader. However, particular projects demand a greater emphasis on the leader's skills, abilities and personal preferences. When comparing his project leaders' performance, one information systems manager commented: 'It seems that John is best suited to closed projects; he likes, and is good at working to our project management methods. But he finds it hard to cope with occasional projects where he has to find his own way through working with people across the organization that he does not know.' We would say that John is good at looking *forwards*, *backwards* and maybe *upwards*, but is not naturally at home with looking *outwards*, *downwards* and *inwards*.

Concrete projects: The conductor of an orchestra

The project leader struggling with a concrete project is like the conductor of an orchestra (Figure 2.5). The situation is very complex, with different highly-qualified instrumentalists to be harmonized, playing to their own highest standards, but in harmony with others. The score is known, each knows his or her part. Nevertheless, there is enormous difference in interpretation and success of the end result: from the original and creative to the mundane or even shambolic. Keeping a sensitive finger on the pulse and taking immediate action based on good judgement, experience and intuition make the difference.

What distinguishes successful leaders of concrete projects is that they prefer:

● to work within a backbone of structure provided by a given set of processes

43

- Makes it work
- Brings parts together
- Finger on the pulse
- Score exists.

Figure 2.5 Concrete projects: The orchestral conductor

- to build a team with people whose expertise they understand – based on education and experience
- to solve problems actively, doing what it takes to get the job done – a trouble-shooter
- to take a high profile, be the visible integrator of communication and activity – the person with whom the buck stops.

Occasional projects: The sculptor

Occasional projects require different strengths. What do sculptors do? They start with a design, maybe a commission: a sketch, or a model (Figure 2.6). So they need to develop a sense of what their output should look like in the context where it will be placed. Their task is to shape, mould, modify as they go along, often according to the nature of the material they are using: the grain of the wood, the structure of the stone or the properties of the metal. What distinguishes successful leaders of occasional projects is that they prefer:

- to integrate a range of different people's perspectives into an evolving output – alliance-builders

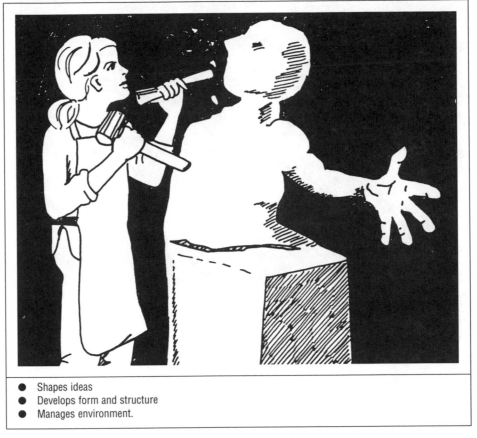

- Shapes ideas
- Develops form and structure
- Manages environment.

Figure 2.6 Occasional projects: The sculptor

- to keep a focus on the output, but be flexible about the steps necessary to achieve it – tolerate ambiguity
- to question the established ways of doing things, and modify or select to suit the situation – pathfinders.

Open projects: The mole

Typically, leaders of open projects are good at much less obvious means of getting things done. What comes to mind when we think of a mole? It's small, dark and hard-working, invisible since its operations are mainly underground, except when the familiar trail of earth mounds erupt across the lawn (Figure 2.7). Likewise, the open project leader tends to prefer:

- to work outside the bright light of the mainstream, pulling resources from wherever, finding space and time where it does not officially exist – underground operator

- Underground
- Finds new ways and tries out
- Pops up from time to time.

Figure 2.7 Open projects: The mole

- to find new ways and means to test ideas, break the mould – an innovator
- to build continued support with a few influencers to maintain the momentum of early successes – informal influencer or entrepreneur.

This range of project leader's preferences may imply what many project leaders have always believed, that they are supposed to be super-heroes. Alternatively it may imply that some project leaders are better suited to some types of project than others, even if they are well trained and experienced in the generic project management skills and strategies. Both project leaders and their bosses need to think about the types of projects they have in their portfolio, and where possible, to match a project to the project leader's preferences. As illustrated here, these preferences will involve more than previous experience or technical capability.

Conclusions

Projects can be classified along a continuum that consists of the extent to which the deliverables can be defined at the outset, the level of structure and formality needed to run a project and the amount of learning the project team and the organization is undertaking. There are, broadly speaking, three types of project: *concrete*, *occasional* and *open*. Each type of project has different characteristics, advantages and disadvantages which need to be understood by project leaders so that they can adjust their leadership role to the project, and use appropriate project structures and tools to manage it.

Each project demands widely varying capabilities in the project leader. An individual's preferred way of working may be better suited to one type of project than another.

Part II
Preparing the ground

In this section the focus is on what you need to do before you start the implementation of your project. Huge numbers of projects fail because project leaders are anxious to be seen to be 'doing' things. They leap into inappropriate actions prematurely. Preparing the ground assiduously is the key to being a wise and successful project leader.

3   Understanding the Big Picture

Projects which are successfully implemented, that have a long operational life and are not expensive to maintain can trace the roots of their success to the groundwork done in the early stages. More time, more involvement of stakeholders, plus step-by-step scoping and planning, builds foundations that are robust and flexible. This supports what we hear about the difference in approach between Japanese and Western businesspeople. It is said that the Japanese spend 80% of their time working out what to do, through active planning and experimentation, with 20% spent on implementation. Westerners spend 20% of their time on planning, usually with a small group of people, with 80% spent on implementation. Compared with the Japanese model, the latter usually takes more time overall, produces a poorer-quality product, with expensive support or add-on costs needed to sort out problems. Occasional and open projects, because of their nature, change direction as they evolve, so a more flexible approach is needed, understanding a project's direction and the options that need to be balanced in order to realize desirable business benefits.

This part of the book investigates the ground that needs to be prepared in order to secure success. The main areas are illustrated in Figure 3.1.

- understanding the Big Picture
- identifying the project risks – both technical and managerial
- managing the sponsor – to build a constructive relationship
- iterative scoping – to establish deliverables and success criteria.

The mountaineer Chris Bonington, speaking of climbing teams, commented:

> It is important that all members of the team feel that they are completely in the picture and trusted. Through their understanding of the overall picture they can contribute to the success of the enterprise.

These sentiments apply equally to all projects, indeed to any activity where a number of people came together for a specific purpose.

Every project needs a Big Picture from which everybody can see what the project is and why it is important. If people do not know the purpose behind a

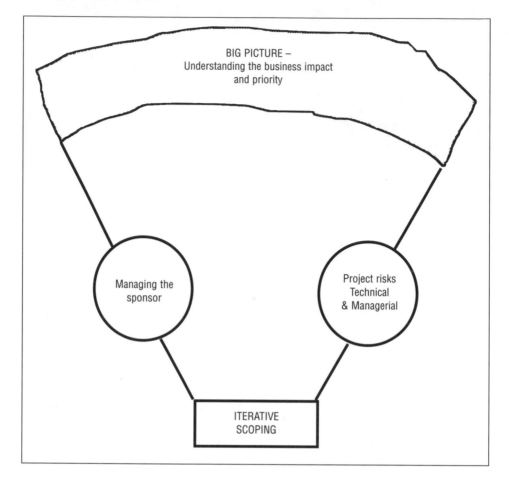

Figure 3.1 Preparing the ground – The main elements

project, it has no meaning for them; their actions have less consequence, so they are less committed to its success. If you want to build a highly-motivated project team, you need a clearly-expressed rationale and purpose. As Ron Buckridge of the CEGB has said: 'Project management is an art, and every artist needs a vision.'

British Airways has a Big Picture. It is the leading airline in the world in an increasingly deregulated industry. A project linked to improving customer service in, say, check-in or seat reservation is a discrete part of a bigger and more important whole. The specific project does not seem isolated or incomprehensible. It is a clear and worthwhile part of a vision, expressed in words that all can understand. If the Big Picture is clear and simple, the project gains a sense of purpose and direction.

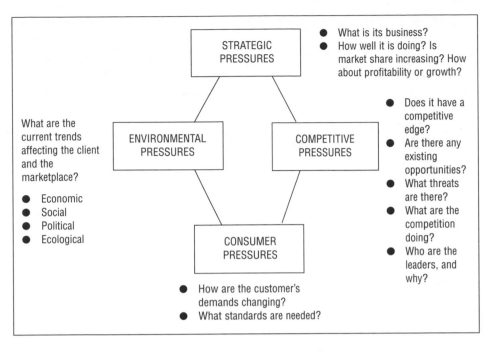

Figure 3.2 Pressures on the client organization

The pressures on the client organization

What drives a project may not at first be easy to see. It is helpful to stand back from the specific project objectives to see why the project is significant to the client organization. Figure 3.2 summarizes the pressures upon the client organization. The Big Picture may be affected by a number of these pressures, or by just one. Let us look briefly at each.

Strategic pressures

These are pressures affecting overall performance. There may be programmes aimed at meeting profit objectives needed for survival or future investment. They may involve improved product development, manufacturing, administration or selling. You need to find out where the company places most emphasis – what is perceived as being vital to the organization's health?

Another strategic pressure felt by many organizations is how to become flexible and fast-moving against a background of traditional, hierarchical and bureaucratic culture. So the aims of a project may include setting up collaborative ways of working, or building effective alliances between organizations. Many joint ventures will only succeed in realizing the mutual benefits of new developing services or products if ways of working together function smoothly.

Everyone knows that the Far East is very competitive and able to produce high-quality goods at low prices. Continuously reducing costs, new production methods to improve quality, increased speed and flexibility are constantly present in all manufacturing organizations there. Standing still, gradually upgrading existing products and marginally reducing costs is not an option. Radical alternatives have to be introduced and then, almost immediately, challenged again as competitors catch up.

As product life cycles shorten, the speed of new product innovation and business renewal is a constant pressure that cannot be ignored. This means that attention has to be paid to improving what we do today whilst planning the products/services of tomorrow. Is your project a radical response to competitive pressure or the company's future? Putting together what you have discovered for yourself and what the client tells you will give you a picture of the pressures which have created the need for your project.

Some supermarket chains have projects which are developing systems to identify and measure the costs of buying, stocking, handling and selling all the items on their shelves. The Big Picture reason for these projects is to manage the mix of products to achieve profit levels which are predictable. Cost margins are narrow and can easily be lost with all supermarkets now offering a wide range of exotic foods, as well as standard items. Some foods are relatively very expensive to buy and handle. To continue to operate, the supermarkets must manage the detailed profitability of individual lines of food and be able to predict which new lines will contribute at what profit level.

Consumer pressures

Consumer pressure may take the form of changing tastes. In the package holiday market, for example, nowadays consumers are not so keen to book the cheapest holiday if it means staying in unfinished hotels. They are becoming more discriminating, and are looking for comfort, excitement and sports facilities, as well as value for money. We are moving out of the 'take it or leave it' era of mass production into an era of customized products and services.

This need to keep up with consumer tastes may be driving new product development or a new campaign for existing products in your client organization. Is the customer important to the Big Picture of your project?

Environmental pressures

It may at first seem that 'the environment' is too broad a concept to relate to a particular project. But it quickly becomes clear that political, social and economic forces can influence the overriding purpose of a project. For instance, the ageing population is creating new waves of activity in housing, leisure, investment and pensions.

Public opinion, as well as legislation, is causing organizations to consider the ecological implications of their products and production methods. Sustainable growth, recyclable materials, environmentally friendly habitats or healthy lifestyles are increasingly becoming part of the context of a project. This wider perspective includes piloting working practices that enable people who are disadvantaged in society to become involved.

How does your organization and your project contribute to these wider perspectives?

The project leader and the Big Picture

Part of the project leader's job is to determine the business context of the project, to identify the sort of impact the deliverables of the project should have – i.e. to find answers to the question: 'How does this project contribute to customer service and our competitive position in the market?'

The answers to this question lead to further questions, such as 'What do we as a project team need to do to ensure the intended business impact?' If you can answer these questions and discuss them convincingly with your project team, you will establish a common project vision on which everybody's attention is focused.

Project types and the Big Picture

In Chapter 2 we introduced the idea of a project continuum, with projects ranging from concrete to open. There is another dimension called *project visibility* which helps you to identify the ways in which your project is important to your organization's Big Picture, and therefore what you have to manage actively as the project leader. Figure 3.3 lists aspects of this dimension. The two continuums may be combined to give a matrix of project types that pose very different management challenges. These can be mapped out and anticipated by the project leader (Figure 3.4).

Concrete projects

The projects that fall on the left hand side of Figure 3.4 are more easily recognized by project leaders. However, the dimension of visibility means that they will pose different degrees and types of risk.

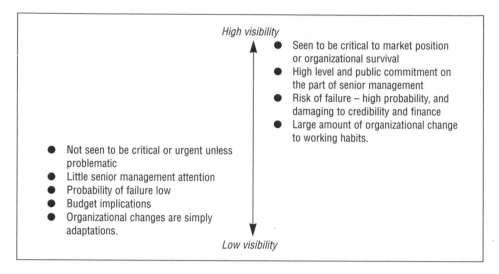

Figure 3.3 Project visibility

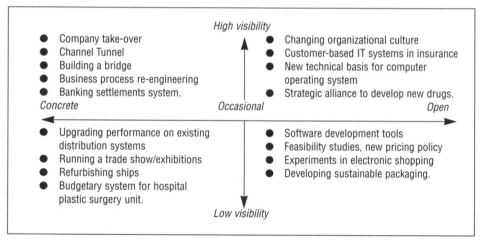

Figure 3.4 Matrix of project types

Concrete – Low-visibility projects

These projects tend to be less critical to the organization. There will be considerable know-how, either in the organization or amongst external experts, so information regarding best practice will be readily available. The project leader who is, for instance, organizing a regular exhibition or trade show will need to pay attention to detailed planning and watch out carefully for dependencies, liaising frequently with contributors of all kinds.

One task is to build and maintain constructive working relationships with all the stakeholders. The background political issues will not usually be crucial, unless something goes dramatically wrong. So on the basis of a clear performance or service 'agreement', the main challenge is face-to-face discussions to co-operatively manage the dependencies, expectations and outputs of the stakeholders. Conflicts, entrenched positions and misunderstood deliverables cause most difficulties.

The risks of this project type tend to be:

● poor previous experience with stakeholders, either users or suppliers
● lack of detailed planning, monitoring and problem-solving
● failure to learn from previous problems, so mistakes are repeated.

Concrete – High–visibility projects

These projects pose many more risks, with potentially greater consequences for the project leader and the organization. Budgets are usually higher, and technically, although a lot may be known there may be several critical aspects that are untested. For instance, a new short-distance ferry vessel may combine many features of existing services, but embarkation layouts and processes may involve new technology and procedures that are untested. If they do not work smoothly the whole service may be discredited in the media, or delays may be experienced before the service can be launched. Careful planning, knowing the critical points and assessing the scale and probability of known risks are essential in these high-profile projects.

However, the organizational politics of this type of project are likely to absorb much of the project leader's time and emotional energy, as they will attract senior management attention and trigger their anxieties, both rational and irrational. Organizational tensions will be heightened by the real and perceived risks. It is likely that significant organizational change or realignment will need to take place if this type of project is to be implemented successfully, so it can be anticipated that resistance – both organizational and individual – will be stimulated and will have to be managed skilfully, and handled formally through the sponsor and the project steering board, but just as importantly, informally by the project leader, through influence and networking.

Managing stakeholders' expectations to ensure that they are realistic and up-to-date, no matter whether the news about the project's progress is good or bad, is a heavyweight job, and the project leader will have to be in the thick of the organization's dynamic political processes.

The risks of this type of project are:

● there is a lack of focus on the critical path of dependencies and they are not made clear to all – so problems are buried and control is lost
● stakeholders run away with unrealistic expectations – either positive or negative
● the political dynamics amongst senior management are not actively and continuously managed to reduce surprises – so in-fighting takes over.

Open projects

On the right hand side of the matrix in Figure 3.4, the management problems and the risks are different. There will tend to be more technical unknowns, either within the organization or perhaps in the world, because there are some genuinely leading-edge aspects. Hence the technical risks may be more unpredictable, either in their consequences or the probability of them occurring.

Open – Low-visibility projects

These projects tend to be low-budget research and development activities, so the consequences of failure are not serious. Usually something constructive comes out of the project, even if it is cancelled in the certain knowledge that this one will not fly.

The project leader needs to take care over how and when successes are made public, in order to gain further support for a bigger project which might still be open but with higher visibility, or concrete and more focused. Going public too soon can create expectations that are then disappointed because the results are unimpressive and do not seem to lead anywhere. Alternatively, surprising senior managers with a proposal that is proven, well advanced and involves big decisions will shake the status quo. Resistance will be triggered and a good idea may be rejected for the wrong reasons.

Typical risks for this type of project are:

- lack of definition of the short, experimental phases – these need to be balanced between casting wide and focusing on something achievable that moves forward
- setting review points that are too far ahead, against criteria that are too woolly – this leads to the project running off, nobody is quite sure where, wasting money, time as well as individuals' enthusiasm
- being seen by the rest of the organization as submissive, because the project is internal and lacks sponsor or key player support

Open – High-visibility projects

For the project leader, these projects are the most unpredictable and prone to failure. Sometimes they are doomed to failure before they start, so the project leader should either refuse the invitation to take on the project or have a well-packed parachute to hand.

The fatal combination that we have encountered several times is political visibility – because the company had publicly committed resources and announced the strategic importance of the venture – combined with a number of risky technical elements, plus a step change in organizational culture amongst stakeholders who have little experience or motivation; this leads to a very lively mixture that may well explode or implode. One example of such a project is the

European Union's history of co-operation to develop High Definition Television: large in scale, competitively important, involving many players with different interests, and several technical options with undesirable trade-offs.

One successful project is the European World Health Organization's 'Healthy Cities Project'. This has generated hundreds of projects in cities across Europe which have brought politicians, environmentalists, transport and housing experts together with medics and the providers of community services to tackle local health priorities.

Typical risks for this type of project are:

● insufficient time and attention paid to leading the stakeholders in a common project direction
● underestimating the scale and difficulty of organizational change – everything needs to be built or rebuilt into the new ways of working
● there are too many risks – if they are considered separately they seem manageable, but when they are put together they are overwhelming
● huge budget overruns with little output caused by a one-off budget.

Figure 3.5 summarizes the different types of projects and what the project leader needs to concentrate on. What is crucial to your project's successful management?

Assessing project risks

Do you know what risks are involved in your project? Did you know before you started the project? What would you have done differently if you had spotted some of the surprises that crept up on you during the project? Perhaps this is the most crucial step in preparing the ground, because if you know the sort of project you are leading, then you, your sponsor and core team members can identify at least 80% of the anticipated risks, and plan contingency actions. Thinking the project through in the early phase has a number of benefits:

● You and your sponsor gain a better understanding of what the project involves, so you start your relationship on a sound footing.
● If you think the project is not viable, you can make a decision regarding the conditions you need to have in place in order to continue, or withdraw from the project, making your reasons clear.
● You can put into place an appropriate planning and decision-making infrastructure that will help to deal with issues as they arise. You might plan a series of workshops with users to define needs and build prototypes with more stakeholder involvement, or you could set up a cluster of exploration task forces, if the project is open and visible.
● You can assess the overall probability of the project failing as a result of

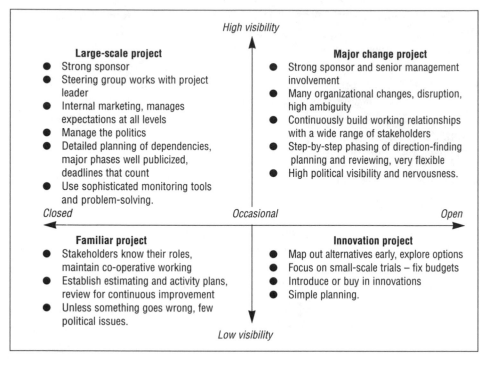

High visibility

Large-scale project
- Strong sponsor
- Steering group works with project leader
- Internal marketing, manages expectations at all levels
- Manage the politics
- Detailed planning of dependencies, major phases well publicized, deadlines that count
- Use sophisticated monitoring tools and problem-solving.

Major change project
- Strong sponsor and senior management involvement
- Many organizational changes, disruption, high ambiguity
- Continuously build working relationships with a wide range of stakeholders
- Step-by-step phasing of direction-finding planning and reviewing, very flexible
- High political visibility and nervousness.

Closed   Occasional   Open

Familiar project
- Stakeholders know their roles, maintain co-operative working
- Establish estimating and activity plans, review for continuous improvement
- Unless something goes wrong, few political issues.

Innovation project
- Map out alternatives early, explore options
- Focus on small-scale trials – fix budgets
- Introduce or buy in innovations
- Simple planning.

Low visibility

Figure 3.5 Project management approaches

traditional risks, such as new technology, natural disasters, the financial instability of a partner, legislative changes or the loss of vital experts.

Where there are high risks, you can start to minimize them at an early stage and devise alternative plans of action, highlighting critical points during the project's life where you might start to see problems occurring. This proactive risk management should run throughout the project life cycle.

Mapping project risks

At an early meeting during project start-up, the project leader, sponsor and some key clients, contributors or suppliers need to map the risks by going through a structured process.

A suggested process
- brainstorm possible risks
- consider what has gone wrong in similar projects previously
- cluster into related topics
- weight – seriousness and probability
- focus on the very serious and highly probable
- define the project type, and review typical risks

- plan how to run the project with the risks in mind. Highlight where in the project the risks will be most critical
- decide how to reduce the risks so that the chances and consequences of failure are minimized.

Checklist of potential project risks

You will need to develop your own checklist for projects in your organization, focusing particularly on the areas where projects typically go wrong in your environment. The checklist in Figure 3.6 (see p. 62) is just a starting point, not a definitive list; it will help you think of some areas you might otherwise overlook. High-visibility projects, particularly open ones, benefit from this mapping exercise. Project leaders need to understand what they have really taken on, at a stage where they can do something, before the focus on the consequences of failure makes it very hard to discuss the options.

Conclusions

All projects are set within the context of an organization and are intended to contribute to its strategic purpose. The project manager needs to understand the trends and forces influencing the Big Picture in order to focus on the project's intended impact. Another dimension needs to be borne in mind – visibility. High-visibility projects are usually expected to make a more important strategic contribution. The dimension of visibility influences the number and scale of project risks. The amount of political attention tends to be greatest for high-visibility projects. The risks and political activity mean that the project manager will have to put effort into managing the stakeholders and the organizational dynamics.

At the start of a project, it is worthwhile for the project leader to assess with the sponsor the project's risks – technical, managerial and organizational. Having weighted and anticipated the risks, then he/she can plan how to handle them. The Scouts' motto, 'Be Prepared', is helpful.

---

1. Business impact & benefits

- strategic impact?
- widely supported?
- quantum leap?
- confidence level?
- cost/benefit expected?

---

2. Project size

- budget?
- deliverables defined?
- time scales and resources?

---

3. Organizational impact

- who is affected? how many? different groups?
- geographical coverage and location?
- level of cultural change?
- legacy of change?
- resistance level?
- level of management involvement? active?
- change in jobs/skills/working practices/relationships/power?
- winners and losers?
- level of preparedness – communication?

---

4. Technical risks & complexity

- new technology – level of experience?
- suitability for purpose, reliability, performance standards?
- knock-on effects?
- reliability of suppliers – technical/commercial?
- nature of relationship?
- interdependencies – number criticality?

---

5. Project management

- brief and expectations?
- sponsorship?
- decision-making process within organization?
- project decision-making?
- appropriate process and methods for defining deliverables?
- project life cycle?
- planning work management?
- resources?
- feedback and feed-forward?
- stakeholder management?

Figure 3.6 Checklist of project risks

4 Managing the sponsor

Different views: The project leader and the sponsor

Joan, the project leader of an information technology (IT) project in a building society, threw her milestone review notes down beside her workstation with a bang. Yet another depressing and frustrating meeting! Blame was hanging heavily in the air. The sponsor, Joan's boss Mark, was clearly angry. He had thought that the project was further ahead than it was. He had not realized that there were serious capability and capacity problems in the network infrastructure that would involve more time and more investment. The business client insisted on adding in new functionality that he claimed was vital to handle a new financial product that would beat their competitors. Joan knew that the project was in crisis; she was being pulled in all directions and the time frames were being compressed. She knew that the team could, and would, deliver something more or less on time, but she knew that the seeds of future crisis were already sown. Her reputation as a project leader was at stake, her feelings of satisfaction in doing a good job had been lost. She would have to survive as best she could, but she knew, as did Mark, that once more the IT department's image for delivering late, inadequate and insufficiently-tested facilities would be reinforced. No wonder she was feeling defeated. 'If only they had told me!' she exclaimed for the umpteenth time. 'If only they would understand and not insist on the impossible,' she continued.

Just across the open plan office, Mark was also letting off steam. 'Why hadn't she told him? Of course he knew that the technical infrastructure was a potential problem, the new hardware and systems were unproven – but *this*! He felt let down. Now he would again have to justify to the Managing Director why the perceived huge investment in IT wouldn't lead to the anticipated business benefits for another 6–12 months. He was coming under more and more pressure in Board Meetings. The IT project was seen by some of his colleagues as the main blockage to significant progress in the business's performance. He was standing on quicksand and it was not much fun!

Project leaders say: 'If only my sponsor was on my side, I would be much more effective.' Conversely, sponsors say: 'If only my project leaders weren't so organizationally and politically clumsy, I wouldn't spend my time bailing them out!' Lose–lose relationships or games are the norm, leading to negative attitudes on both sides. Sometimes the sponsor and project leader are just distant and formal; at worst, they are adversarial. Like Joan and Mark, who are heading for mutual disappointment (which is only one step from mutual blame) this is a poor basis for problem-solving.

Before considering how this central relationship can be made to work effectively let's examine the negative attitudes on both sides. They may be portrayed in the following way.

Sponsor's negative attitudes

- Those technical specialists who become project leaders never understand the realities of organizational life. They talk technicalities and details, they complicate things and fail to see the wider impact of their actions. Their language is foreign to me.
- They assume that I know everything and have the answers and can give them the clarity they want. It's not that easy: I don't have all the answers.
- They never listen. Their immediate reaction is 'It can't be done.' They are inflexible, always on the defensive.
- Things never come out as they say they will. They always hide the bad news or an embarrassing surprise. I never know where it will come from, but I can be certain that come it will!

Project managers' negative attitudes

- The sponsors *must* know what they want, so why don't they just say so, instead of holding back.
- If they do not know what they want, then they must be incompetent.
- If they just tell me what they want, our job is to do it (whatever it is).
- They don't show any consideration for what we have already done when they change their minds. They just criticize, discounting our efforts and expertise.
- They want the impossible and won't listen to reality. We never get any support when we need it most, but ultimately they are responsible.

These mutually reinforcing attitudes lead to a predictable set of interactions. Project briefings or start-up meetings dealing with deliverables and constraints have the flavour of positioning and bargaining. Anticipated risks are not discussed; rather, individuals are asked to make instant choices and commit themselves blind. Already the atmosphere is anything but collaborative – you would think that the parties were on opposite sides. Follow-up meetings tend to be infrequent, so personal contact only takes place in formal arenas. Milestone reviews have a ritualistic flavour: the emphasis is on highlighting good news, featuring progress whilst skilfully avoiding problems. Finally, either at delivery stage or uncomfortably close to it, the project's problems are exposed in a dramatic crisis, followed by disillusionment, acrimonious wrangling and dented careers. Nobody wins. The circle will be repeated in the next project unless this bleak picture can be seen from a different perspective.

Building a constructive relationship with the sponsor – The ingredients

The sponsorship role is much misunderstood by sponsors and project leaders alike, so it needs to be made explicit. What do you need from your sponsor? What can you expect? What does the project look like from their perspective?

This chapter will give you an outline of what the sponsorship role can be, so that you can start to manage upwards to encourage your sponsor to do what the project needs.

It is important to understand the sponsor's perspective. Can you put yourself into the sponsor's chair in order to see and feel the situation they are in? Remember they are human. They have fears, weaknesses, preferences in style and touchy points, just like you or anybody else.

The final ingredient is the project leader's capability to operate effectively in the turbulent organizational dynamics often called 'organizational politics'. Politics is a normal means of peacefully resolving differences or conflicts. Projects, as temporary organizational vehicles, always herald some changes. These will create disturbances at a personal, collective departmental and organizational level, so there will always be unexpected realignments to be negotiated and tried out. Some people will lose, some will resist and some will change easily, but there will always be a complex web of new or different relationship patterns to be unravelled if the project is to be successfully implemented with sustained impact.

The question of sponsorship will be considered in relation to the project types outlined in Chapter 3 to highlight the sort of sponsorship involvement which is necessary for each project type.

The sponsor's role

As the person in the middle who desires the positive results of the project within the usual constraints of time and budget, the sponsor is not responsible for the execution of the project. That is the project leader's job. In this middle position, the sponsor has to look in two or three directions, including outwards to the

65

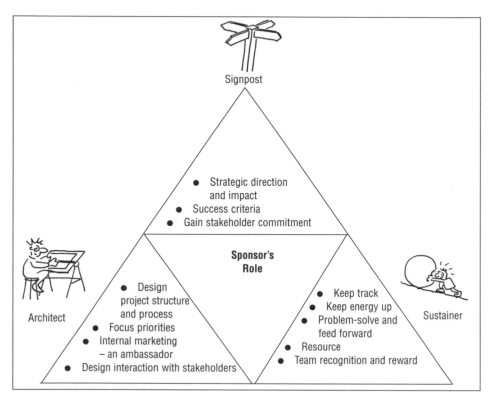

Figure 4.1 A sponsor's role

client. The client may be internal or external, but the sponsor's task is the same – to help define the business impact of the project in the context of the Big Picture. Sponsors need to sense changes, or shifts of emphasis that will influence the project, especially if it is highly visible. This means heavy involvement in the project, at early stages of scoping. During the project, it means internal marketing, managing the politics, door-opening, networking and problem-solving to make sure that the organizational climate around the project is healthy.

The inward-looking facet of the sponsor's role is to ensure that the project leader understands the project's vision and that he/she anticipates the shifting goal-posts, scoping and re-scoping when necessary. The sponsor needs to establish the project type, identifying the inherent risks, the most appropriate project structure, planning and monitoring methods plus resourcing, problem-resolution and decision-making mechanisms. Figure 4.1 outlines the three elements of the role.

The Signpost involves:

- ensuring all the main stakeholders understand the strategic direction and anticipated impact
- helping to relate the project's purpose to the organizational Big Picture

- answering the questions: 'Why are we doing this?' 'What should it look like in the end?' and 'How do we know we are successful?'
- helping to clarify risks, identifying emergent gaps
- negotiating with stakeholders regarding their level of input and involvement.

The Architect concentrates on:

- representing the project to senior management and clients, undertaking active internal marketing
- designing with the project leader the most effective structure and processes to run the project
- designing with the project leader the most suitable approach to stakeholder involvement to ensure that they are continuously integrated into the project life cycle. This might involve deciding on sub-projects, task forces or a series of workshops.

The Sustainer's focus is on:

- keeping the project on track, as the person who is outside, maintaining the wider perspective and anticipating next steps
- keeping the project team energetic and healthy, monitoring the overall programme with the project leader, and recognizing the team's and individuals' achievements at milestone points
- keeping feedback information flowing to the project leader from all aspects of the project, to concentrate on identifying and solving problems as soon as they emerge, emphasizing a feed-forward perspective, asking: 'What should we do differently?'

Contact with the sponsor

We have noticed that both sponsors and project leaders think that their contact with each other should be minimized. Frequent meetings imply failure, or that there are many issues that need to be resolved. Unfortunately, infrequent contact is only appropriate for low-visibility projects, where the project leader and sponsor have worked together frequently for a long time. In these cases the project initiation process may be rapid, based on past success and much joint experience.

An arm's-length relationship will make any high-visibility project more risky for both the sponsor and project leader. Indeed, it may jeopardize the whole project. Both parties have new roles that sometimes sit at odds with traditional line management. The mental model commonly held in people's minds about hierarchical relationships is that the more senior manager delegates tasks clearly to a more junior expert, who then executes the task competently. In flatter, more flexible organizations, structures with these boundaries are eroded, so a new collaborative relationship needs to be built. Both partners have to work together,

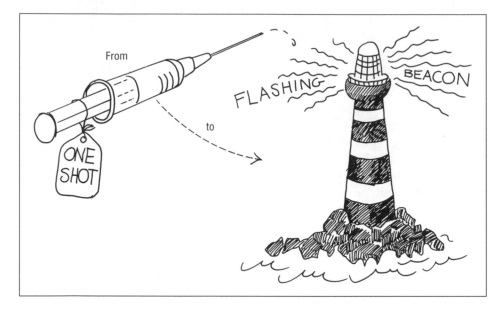

Figure 4.2 Contact with sponsor

with some areas of specifically separate responsibilities, and other areas where they overlap. In these overlapping areas, they have to decide together what to do and how to do it.

In organizations where projects are the way work is delivered, sponsors often take a hands-off position, because they assume that the established procedures for project management should cope with everything except a significant disruption. However, the trend towards more open, smaller projects that are more volatile means that there is a need for a much closer working relationship. Figure 4.2 symbolizes the changing nature of the relationship, particularly for high-visibility open projects. In practical terms, a collaborative relationship means recognizing the 'real' situation that both parties face. In open and high-visibility projects there will be many unknowns, coming from many different directions. As the project progresses there will be new dilemmas, trade-offs to make and new issues to deal with. No single formula or project methodology can guarantee a safe journey through the rough seas. Only by working together can the sponsor and project leader jointly sail a zig-zag course. Bearing this in mind, it helps to see the perspectives of the sponsor and project manager as complementary (Figure 4.3).

The sponsor's dilemmas

The sponsor has a difficult position between the project team and the client. It is a balancing act. One executive who was taking on the sponsor role in an

Sponsor's perspective	Project manager's perspective
• There are some things that I am clear about in this project. I will push hard for these and make sure the project leader knows what is important and why. • There are aspects that are new, there are open questions. I don't have answers, I am not even sure of the questions. We need to identify these open areas together and work on how to find out • There are some organizational, politically sensitive aspects. I need to talk to the project manager, so that *we* can steer around them. • I need to know the problems and be sure the project manager is keeping me up-to-date with progress and problems. I want to understand the project team's views	• I understand that some things are given as far as the sponsor is concerned but others are open, particularly if this is an 'open' project in which we have little experience. • I can raise the problems and predictable constraints in a neutral and well formulated way so that they are taken into account and I do not feel incompetent for not having managed on my own. • The sponsor has a wider organizational perspective. How well tuned-in am I to these aspects? • If I work together with the sponsor we can manage the organizational impact and the problems of the project.

Figure 4.3 The complementary perspectives: Sponsor and project manager

insurance company that was moving towards management said: 'Well, it's like being between the devil and the deep blue sea, negotiating your way like Odysseus through the Straits of Messina.' For each project there are always a number of dimensions that have to be mapped, agreed and actively balanced (Figure 4.4).

Building the relationship

Managing is a two-way activity – sponsors manage downwards and project leaders upwards. With some of the ideas previously discussed in mind, the next step is to actively build a relationship that is mutually respectful and engenders trust. So how do you go about nurturing a collaborative relationship?

Establishing the relationship

If this is a new sponsor, what do you know about them? There is some background work to be done, to find out what the sponsor is like as a person, and what their management style is. From what you know or have heard, how do they like to be informed? Perhaps they are most at home with a quick updating chat, or perhaps they like to be presented with a comprehensive written document. It is also worth reflecting on what you would think was important, how you would distinguish a good project manager from a bad one if you were in their position.

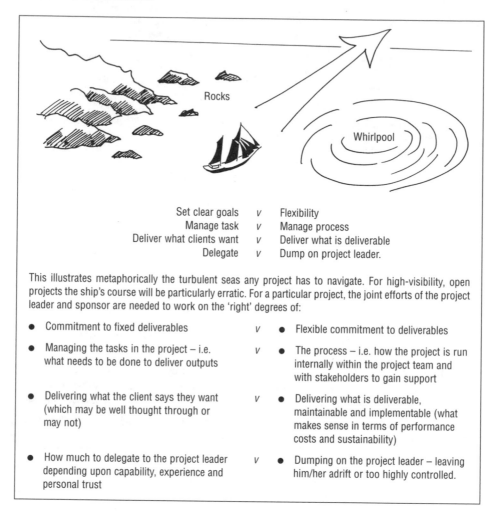

	v	
Set clear goals	v	Flexibility
Manage task	v	Manage process
Deliver what clients want	v	Deliver what is deliverable
Delegate	v	Dump on project leader.

This illustrates metaphorically the turbulent seas any project has to navigate. For high-visibility, open projects the ship's course will be particularly erratic. For a particular project, the joint efforts of the project leader and sponsor are needed to work on the 'right' degrees of:

● Commitment to fixed deliverables	v	● Flexible commitment to deliverables
● Managing the tasks in the project – i.e. what needs to be done to deliver outputs	v	● The process – i.e. how the project is run internally within the project team and with stakeholders to gain support
● Delivering what the client says they want (which may be well thought through or may not)	v	● Delivering what is deliverable, maintainable and implementable (what makes sense in terms of performance costs and sustainability)
● How much to delegate to the project leader depending upon capability, experience and personal trust	v	● Dumping on the project leader – leaving him/her adrift or too highly controlled.

Figure 4.4 Sponsorship dilemmas – The Straits of Messina

Once you have formed a preliminary picture in your mind of the sponsor, it is worth asking yourself: 'What do I need from my sponsor to enable me to be successful in this project?'

Early meetings

This is the point at which the basis of the relationship throughout the whole project becomes established. Remember that the way things begin prejudices how they continue. If you get off on the wrong foot, then it is hard to recover. Rather like fixing a doctor's appointment, there are times when you need to demand a double time slot!

In the meeting, focus the discussion on both your and the sponsor's views of:

- the type of project and the risks expected
- how the project should be run
- conflicting priorities
- 'what if' scenarios to agree how to handle things
- what you want from each other, such as information, support, meetings, early warning signals, and specifically who should do what in the project.

To do this the project leader needs to use plenty of open and probing questions to render underlying assumptions transparent. This is a dialogue, not receiving instructions. Watch how the sponsor reacts – are there non-verbal clues that indicate hesitation, lack of real agreement or discomfort? Check out what is behind these responses. Finally, summarize verbally, or if necessary in writing what has been agreed, what is left open for further discussion or what requires additional information. With open projects there may be several phases of clarification and weighing of alternatives before decisions are reached. This ambiguity can cause unease because it appears that no progress is being made, but it is a most important step, as collaboration starts here through clear and common understanding. You are in it together, for better or worse.

Keeping going

Once the project is launched and rolling, the emergent issues are the major worry, so it is important to ensure that the sponsor knows the good and bad news as soon as possible. No bad surprises – even if the message is hard to deliver. If this ground rule is practised then the project manager and sponsor can:

- deal with the politics of problems before they are overtaken by them
- prepare alternative ways forward to re-plan or renegotiate deliverables in a calmer atmosphere, rather than tense panic.

The main project leadership skills involve gathering the evidence necessary to explain a problem's scale and shape in a straightforward manner. Resist the temptation to find an immediate solution to problems before you have either understood them or considered alternatives. The overriding ability is to listen with patience to what is being said, not what you want to hear.

Managing the politics

Many a project leader longs to be left alone to get on with the project. 'Company politics are nothing to do with me, I just try to avoid them', is a statement from the heart of many a project leader. Engaging actively with the sponsor feels like the first step into the political quagmire. If the project is a high-visibility one, then the changes will stimulate political dynamics, and dealing with them is part of the project leader's job.

What is politics?

Politics can be defined as the peaceful settlement of difference. Politics also has negative connotations, but writers such as Ralph Stacey would argue that they are a necessary, complex and irrational part of organizational life. Organizations are composed of people, structures and process, and people are emotional, irrational beings. Everybody is emotionally involved with the organization in which they work, so they will react to disturbances of their patterns of work, ways of thinking and beliefs about how things should be. As a project leader you cannot avoid involvement in the politics that projects will set in motion, but you may be unaware of how the particular patterns of political activity manifest themselves with your organization. You need to understand how you currently react to these, and choose to learn to respond differently. Ask yourself in which political situations do you feel uncomfortable or out of your depth. How do you deal with them? Who is effective in these situations, and what do they do?

Ability to read political dynamics

Figure 4.5 gives guidelines on some aspects of political behaviour. The horizontal dimension describes an individual's ability to read the political dynamics of their organization: how clearly do you understand and appreciate:

- how informally things are done?
- what decisions are made or avoided?
- what really matters – despite what is publicly said?
- what happens in practice – why do events turn out in a particular way?
- what patterns of behaviour – resisting or enabling – are repeated?
- what are the taboos or undiscussable topics?
- who is the most powerful or influential voice in the organization?

Every organization has its own distinctive answers to these questions. If you are well tuned-in to these dynamics and see what occurs as part of a repeated pattern, not just a chance event aimed randomly at you, then you are in a better position to work out what to do.

The vertical dimension refers to the sort of game-playing that you will usually be involved in borrowing from Eric Berne's Transactional Analysis, which suggests that we each have a life position – a fundamental view of ourself combined with our view of others, which influences our behaviour. We can use this model to reflect on our own behaviour in an organizational context and to try to read others – the sponsor's, for instance. So which are you nearest to – the Sheep, Elephant, Monkey or Owl? In which situations?

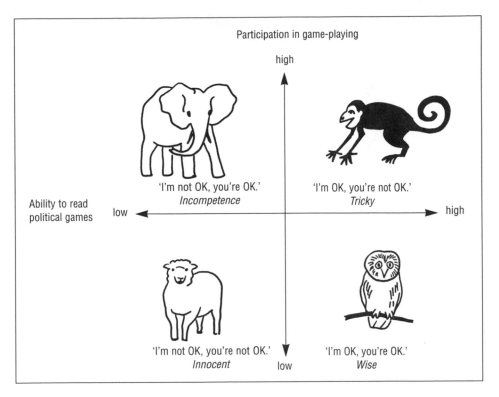

Figure 4.5 Nature of political dynamics – A combination of Kim James's model and Transactional Analysis

Sheep: Innocent – 'I'm not OK, you're not OK.'

Typical Sheep views are:

- 'What politics? Just leave me alone to get on with the work.'
- 'I am not interested in power, because I do not want to fight.'
- 'If I do fight I will probably lose, so I will wait and see what happens.'
- 'What do you mean I should have seen it coming?'

Elephant: Incompetent – 'I'm not OK, you're OK.'

Typical Elephant views are:

- 'What do you mean I walked in and dug a hole for myself?'
- 'I just told it the way it is.'
- 'If they don't understand, don't blame me.'
- 'It's unfair, it's all a fix, they hold all the cards.'

Monkey: Tricky – 'I'm OK, you're not OK.'

Typical Monkey views are:

- 'They're so slow (stupid) I'll get them where I want them.'
- 'They can't catch me; I'm several moves ahead.'
- 'It's all sewn up; wait until they find out!'

Owl: Wise – 'I'm OK, you're OK.'

Typical Owl views are:

- 'I know what's going on here, how can I find a win–win way?'
- 'Let's focus on what we are trying to do and why.'
- 'Wait for the right moment, and it will emerge.'

Once you have worked out where you are in the political environment of your project, you can work out how you work with pivotal stakeholders:

- What do you need to do at which phase in this project?
- How comfortably does this sit with your preferred approach to politics?
- What can you ask your sponsor to do?

Conclusion

The relationship between project leader and sponsor is very different from that of line manager and subordinate. This frequently leads to misunderstandings that have a negative effect on project performance. In the case of open and high-visibility projects, it is vital that the two parties work well together in a robust relationship to manage the unknowns. A durable relationship needs:

- to be built on mutual respect for the difference in roles, project perspectives and the need for continual contact
- to be negotiated at the start of the project to agree mutual expectations and ways of working, and reviewed and renegotiated as the project progresses
- to deal explicitly with the dilemmas inherent in the project
- to work out how to engage constructively with the organizational politics that are an integral part of the project.

5   Scoping

Damaged at birth

A large insurance company suffered from a failure to achieve clarity and commitment to a major business change project. Faced with enormous new competitive pressures and changes in its marketplace, it was forced to examine the effectiveness of its sales force. The Board conceived a major project which involved a radical overhaul of its whole approach to selling, requiring a much more commercial approach to profitability. Amongst many other things, this involved far-reaching changes in the roles and management structures in the sales force, with huge implications for Personnel policy and information systems.

The Board's terms of reference were communicated via a project manager to sub-project managers in the Personnel and Information Technology (IT) departments. It only emerged later that each of these interpreted the project brief and purpose in quite different ways, as did the overall project manager, who came from a sales background. All parties including the Board assumed that the briefs were clear, and each sub-project went to work energetically. In reality, the IT sub-project saw it as just another management information system which had to be interfaced with current systems, whilst the Personnel sub-project saw it as a strategy to make some of the 'old guard' redundant, re-train some people and carry out minor revisions to current pay scales. The Board and the Sales Director saw it as nothing less than a revolution in the company's whole commercial approach which would determine the ability of the business to survive in many of its traditional markets.

The commercial risks were felt to be massive, and the political sensitivity in relation to critical investment analysts as seen as 'self-evident', factors that none of those in IT or Personnel appreciated. It was nearly a year into the three-year project before these fault lines in the project's scoping began to reveal themselves, as IT and Personnel project members who were looking at interfaces in the payment system realized that they had been going down different tracks.

Why undertake scoping?

Sigmund Freud would undoubtedly have enjoyed analysing the situation outlined above, for he would conclude, as have many others who are involved in the project world, that many project problems derive from a traumatic birth or a troubled early childhood. Many of those problems stem from the fundamental relationship between the project sponsor (the parent, if you like) and the project manager. Later project problems most frequently stem from a lack of clarity, agreement or commitment by key players in the organization to the fundamental aims of the project.

Scoping is the process through which clarity, agreement and commitment are obtained. That is its overt purpose. However, it also has the covert purpose of helping the key players in the organization to rehearse mentally what the implications of the project might be, how these might affect the project definition, and how they might be anticipated and prepared for. This covert purpose has many similarities to ideas of 'mental rehearsal' which are now widely used in the field of sports psychology. The act of imagining the whole cycle of a project, anticipating what can be expected and what might be the unexpected, helps to iron out problems before they occur, rather as a pilot may learn to deal with many different situations in a flight simulator.

The covert purpose of scoping

Project managers in particular need to realize that other important objectives are being achieved and judgements made during the process of project scoping. On the positive side, gathering contributions from different stakeholders and collectively anticipating problems is the crucial element in building a team of people committed to the project. It also serves to resolve conflicts and to help all these people become more clear about what they really want to achieve, rather than what they *thought* they wanted to achieve. The second positive function is to enable the project manager and the project team to gain sufficient understanding of the complexities involved in the project that they rapidly increase their chances of success. Such a depth of understanding of the project's implications is also an important prerequisite to enabling the project manager and senior management sponsor to make a credible and persuasive bid for the resources required. At the same time, throughout the scoping process the project manager is either building or destroying people's confidence in him/her and his/her credibility to handle the issues. At this early stage, key players are making judgements about the project's chances of success.

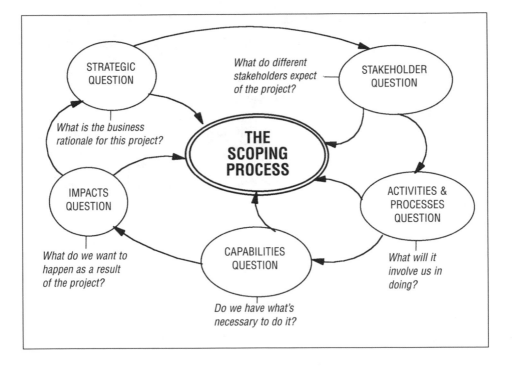

Figure 5.1 The five critical questions

The five critical questions

Figure 5.1 provides a structured approach to the scoping process by posing five critical questions that need to be answered as you start to prepare the ground.

What is the business rationale for the project?

As projects become a more and more widely-used vehicle in organizations, so there arise problems concerning their relevance to the business. They emerge in all sorts of ways – the Chairman may have thought it up in the bath, or it may be the product of painstaking research or endless committee discussions. In practice, we find a major problem to be the plethora of projects which are the whim of some individual or department and which cannot in truth be seen as priorities related to the strategy or vision of the organization.

Project managers therefore need to be both wary and courageous in asking questions regarding relevance and rationale. The simplest way of doing this is to ask those with a stake in the project: 'Why do you want it?' Their answers will reveal very rapidly whether this is a mainstream activity or not.

What do different stakeholders expect of the project?

Even where the business rationale has been well established, there will still be many different views within the organization of what the project has to deliver for the business. An important element in the scoping process is to establish who the various stakeholders (i.e. those with some sort of expectations of the project) are. The first step is to brainstorm with your sponsor, and perhaps with one or two other interested parties, to decide who the various stakeholders in the project might be. We call this 'stakeholder mapping'. It is an important tool for project managers in a number of different areas, including scoping and internal marketing (see Chapter 7). The tool is described in more detail later on in this chapter.

You then have to go out and talk to all of these people and develop the necessary interviewing and probing skills which will enable you to draw out of them what their expectations are. In practice, at this very early stage, these stakeholders are most unlikely to be clear about what they want. Your job is to engage in a dialogue with them to help them to think through their expectations, and to begin to point out where different expectations may conflict with each other. At this stage it is also important that you challenge one-track thinking about solutions. It is vital to explore alternatives if the real problem is to be solved.

What will it involve us in doing?

Your sponsor and stakeholders will frequently be somewhat anxious about a new project at this early stage, particularly where it is an open project characterized by considerable ambiguity and uncertainty. What they are really looking for as a result of the scoping process is at least a rough idea of what kinds of activities might be necessary in order to complete the project. They need to know what the organization is letting itself in for. Whilst there is no way that you can produce detailed plans at this stage (you're simply not advanced enough in your thinking), what you *can* do is to begin to sketch out some of the broad activity areas in conjunction with other people who may have a contribution to the project. Some of these activities will emerge from your deliberations quite clearly. Other areas will be very vague – for example, where there is little previous experience within the organization. This question also helps different people to think widely about the implications of what is being proposed.

Do we have what's necessary to do it?

Your initial consideration of stakeholder expectations and activity areas will help you to begin to understand the kinds of resources the project might require. When we talk about resources, we do not only mean the obvious tangible resources of money, time and materials, we also mean those intangible resources of technical skills, non-technical managerial and communications skills, and the vital intangible of commitment and support from particular people within the organization and outside it. What you are really doing is assessing where the organization may have capability gaps and where the areas of difficulty in delivering aspects of the project may lie.

What do we want to happen as a result of the project?

Traditional project management thinking focuses on inputs and outputs, or deliverables. We have come to believe that this type of thinking is inadequate for projects within organizations and is one of the main causes of failure or disappointment. We know of projects, for example, set up to develop a training programme for project leaders. The project group set to with gusto, interviewing project managers about their needs, and then began to define deliverables such as training materials, training programmes and overhead slides which would be required to run training courses. Nobody thought to ask the questions: 'Why do we want to train these project managers? What is the impact we want to have on the organization as a result of their training?' In reality, the desired impact was to change the organization's whole approach to managing multiple projects. Once this was realized it became clear that not only were training outputs required for project managers, but also activities to educate senior managers in their role of managing a multiple-project situation, and new information systems to keep track of simultaneous projects needed to be developed. This had to be combined with a large-scale communications exercise reaching out to everybody within the department so that they understood what was happening.

This consideration of impact rather than tangible deliverables helped the team to redefine the scope of their project substantially, and indeed to satisfy the multiple stakeholders considerably more. You should therefore *start* by considering your project's desired impact on the organization and then work backwards to consider what kinds of deliverables would achieve that.

Iterative scoping

You will now see clearly how consideration of impact brings you full circle back to the strategic question of the business rationale for the project. Particularly with open projects, you may find that you need to go round the cycle of the five questions a number of times, each cycle gradually refining and clarifying everybody's concept of what the project will involve, until it is sufficiently concrete that you can sensibly make detailed plans about how to implement it. This process we call 'iterative scoping'. It is a fundamental approach even for apparently clear, concrete projects. The reality is that even clear terms of reference are interpreted and manipulated differently by different stakeholders.

Iterative scoping is the process that not only builds clarity and a common picture, but crucially, also builds the commitment of the key players to the success of the project. Time taken at this stage – although many will say it's taking too long – will pay handsome dividends later in shortening the implementation process.

Making the case

Once you have this overview of your project you are in a strong position to make the case for it to be properly resourced and supported.

How to justify resources

- *Make a good case* 'If I understand their reasoning and have the impression that they have thought the issues through, then I am likely to believe their budgets', was the advice of one sponsor who had to decide how to allocate limited resources between several projects. There are two parts to making a good case. First, show that the basis of the estimates is reasonable. This means that if you have used firm historical data you must say so, and illustrate the risks that you have experienced in the past due to arbitrary cuts. Or if your project is at the open end of the continuum, you must indicate that this is a best guess, which will be reviewed after certain events have clarified the resource demands. It helps to demonstrate that you have consulted others thought to be sound, when you were putting your case together. Second, make your information easy for the sponsor to understand, using simple graphical summaries where possible. Masses of detail that looks unstructured does not give the sponsor confidence that the project is in good hands.
- *Be credible to the stakeholders* Knowing the Big Picture and being familiar with the political network of the organization will help you to present your case. Highlight aspects that you believe will be seen as important in the wider company context. You can afford to push hard on these, whilst soft-pedalling on demands likely to be perceived by others as less important. Showing that you understand the trade-offs that have to be made between high- and low-visibility projects will earn you respect in your sponsor's eyes.
- *Know when to be flexible* Even the most genial people can become obstinate and difficult when it comes to budgets. The adversarial approach rarely gains the best outcome, but that doesn't mean you have to fall over in the face of opposition. You must choose your cause. When resource reduction seriously threatens you, then you must resist. However, you must also show that you are aware of other issues which management will be taking into consideration. For instance, try to suggest solutions to resource problems as well as just stating what you need. One project manager, in an opera company,

found that she was asking for a certain stage technician's time when he was involved in rehearsals for another production. She suggested a way in which her proposed schedule could be altered so that he could join her production team too.

- *Intangible resources* Other projects and departments will be fighting equally hard to obtain resources. To be sure of securing those you require, you therefore need to draw on your own intangible resources – the confidence, trust, ideas and active support of individuals outside your visible team, whether they are sponsors or invisible team members in other departments, such as finance, marketing or personnel. Your own network and credibility within it will help you to gain support when you most need it. You will have to be prepared to help others out. Intangible resources work on an informal basis of mutual give and take. ('Oh yes, I think I can get Fred to do that, he owes me a good turn.') Find routes through your network of contacts, tapping into resources to find different approaches to getting things done. With temporary, and especially with open projects, intangible resources will be your main resource bank. Build and nurture them. They have a high yield.

Mistaken beliefs about scoping

Whether your project is a concrete one (where there is considerable previous experience within the organization) or an open one, where there is little previous experience in the organization (particularly where the project concerns bringing about change within the organization), there are a number of frequent mistakes that project managers and their senior management sponsors make at the early stages. These stem from a number of erroneous beliefs.

- the belief that senior managers give a lot of thought to what they want from a project before they give it to the project leader
- the belief that the senior manager's definition of the problem or solution should be accepted because he/she has thought about it or has more experience
- the belief by senior managers that what is obvious to them must be obvious to the project leader or project team
- the belief that project clients ought to have a clear idea of what they want
- the belief that if the terms of reference are in writing they will be understood.

All too frequently, the result of these beliefs is disappointment among sponsors and clients, disillusionment among project leaders and teams, and recrimination and scapegoating (the search for the guilty party).

Tools for Scoping

There is no standard methodology for scoping, but there are a number of techniques and skills that can be useful, which we now describe briefly. Use these selectively to begin with, and gradually expand your skills as you try out different approaches. We call them 'the tools for scoping'.

Stakeholder mapping

All those who have a significant contribution to make to the success of the project must be seen by the project leader as part of the team, because they are the stakeholders on whom lasting success depends. You perhaps need to think of 'contribution' in a wider sense than usual. People contribute not only through their special skills and expertise, but also through being supportive and by expressing their expectations clearly. The project leader's task is to establish the different types of contribution needed and the impact of each one, and to devise ways of mobilizing all the contributions towards the same end.

It is helpful to have a simple map linking the principal stakeholders. Every such map will show a unique pattern, but some features have been found to appear frequently and Figure 5.2 illustrates a familiar sort of pattern. Anybody who appears on a map like this is a member of the project's organizational team.

The three broad groups are:

- internal stakeholders
- customer stakeholders (who may be internal or external)
- external stakeholders (other than customers).

We now consider each of these groups in terms of the different interests they have in a project, and their relative importance in your team.

Internal stakeholders

We have identified four main categories of internal stakeholder:

- *The project leader* He or she wants the project to be successful, aims to be effective and competent, and will want to maintain a good reputation within the organization.
- *The core members* These are the regular contributors, who may be full- or part-time, each of whom has a particular skill. They are seen by themselves and others to be formally associated with the project. They are usually the visible team. They want sufficient scope and resources to do a good job and make the project a success, and thus gain personal satisfaction.
- *The sponsor* This is the senior manager, who fosters, guards and promotes the project, but is not directly involved in operational details. The sponsor is primarily concerned, if the project is an internal one, to maintain credibility

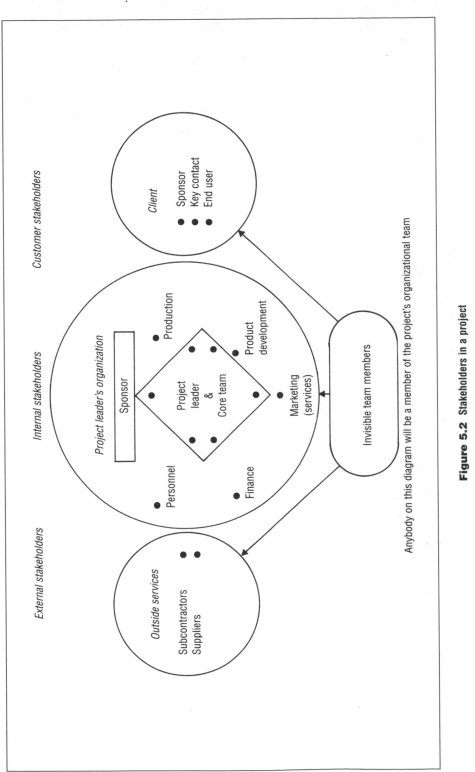

Figure 5.2 Stakeholders in a project

Anybody on this diagram will be a member of the project's organizational team

and currency within the organization, but he or she may also have personal ideas or interests which need to be taken into account. If the project is for an external client, the sponsor has the organization's interests uppermost and is concerned with costs and reputation.

- *The other members* These can be described as the suppliers of services which are part of the project. They are frequently specialists who give advice or administrative support, usually in other departments such as Finance, Personnel, Computing, Distribution and Secretarial. They are interested to know when and to what extent their services will be required. But most of all they want to understand enough about the project to be able to deliver to the best of their abilities.

Customer stakeholders (external or internal)

Every type of project has an ultimate customer or client. The expectations of the customer may be clear or confused, but it is the customer who accepts or rejects the project team's output. Customers are becoming more demanding in terms of acceptable quality of products and services, so even when you know your customer well you cannot be complacent.

In a project for an external client, the most powerful stakeholder is the individual who holds the purse strings. He/she is concerned about the nature of the project, its broad business applications, and the kind of organization you represent. Sometimes it is much more complex: there may be a steering group representing multiple stakeholders in the client organization. As well as the decision-makers, there are often end users whose operations may be significantly affected by the results of a project. The perspective of such people at the sharp end may be very different from that of senior management. For instance, the laboratory technician who administers a medical diagnostic kit will have very different concerns from the doctor who prescribed the test, or the hospital or governmental purchasing agent who decided to make the test available. But the technician's feelings may not be known to the decision-makers.

Many projects are for internal clients – i.e. for other departments or companies under the umbrella of the same organization. A common example is the computer department which develops bespoke software for the marketing, finance or distribution department of the same company. Internal clients deserve the same care and attention as external clients. Assumptions based on historical prejudice are often made about other departments and these have to be challenged. Users will have different perspectives and interests which need to be understood and taken into account. It is easier to show this understanding if the customer stakeholders are at the very least perceived as team members, and better still, become actual members of the team.

External stakeholders

There are many different kinds of external stakeholders. Some of the most common are suppliers of raw materials and products, specialist advisers or consultants, subcontractors and third parties who do part of the work, governmental bodies who execute statutory requirements as inspectors, interest groups, lobbyists, voluntary group opinion leaders and the media.

There exists an 'adversarial' view in which all those inside an organization are seen to have common interests which are not shared by those outside it and are likely to be opposed by them. Organizational networking fundamentally challenges the adversarial view. It does not deny that there are conflicts of interest, but it approaches them as problems to be worked through, by building robust links with outsiders on the basis that there are benefits to be gained by all involved. Instances where suppliers or subcontractors have been brought in to work closely with the project team show that the speed and quality of communication, and therefore appropriate action, increases dramatically. The message is to bring in from the cold the main outside players, work continuously with them and not against them, and ensure that they work with you.

All external stakeholders have one thing in common: their ability to make your project a success or a failure. You need to bring them on board and harness their power.

Interviewing skills

How do you find out what the business rationale for a project is when people themselves may not be very clear? How do you find out what stakeholders want from the project when they haven't had much time to give it thought? The answer lies in being very skilful during the interviewing process. The first step is to know how to develop rapport with the people you are interviewing to help them feel at ease and to explain to them broadly what the interview is about and why you are doing it. The second step lies in the quality of the questions that you ask. At this early stage it is very important to ask open questions (those that illicit an elaborating response from your interviewee) rather than closed questions (those that just illicit a yes or no answer). You also need to become skilful at listening for small clues, sometimes disguised, which if probed and investigated further might lead to useful information. You have to be a little bit like a detective or an archaeologist, gradually working your way through irrelevant information to get at that which is really important to the individual. This requires interviewing skills such as summarizing, probing and asking for concrete examples as a way of helping people to articulate more clearly what they are after.

Success criteria

Success criteria are used by stakeholders to judge how well you are doing. Understanding the different bases for their judgements will stand you in good stead, for they are rarely as simple as they seem.

As we have seen, there are concrete projects where the output and the success criteria can be clearly defined (for example, the development of a new aircraft to meet specific operational requirements). At the other end of the spectrum are problem-solving or open projects whose purpose may be to define a desirable output. In such a case the main success criteria are likely to be the desires/ambitions of the individual stakeholders, which cannot necessarily be measured at the outset. For example, a project team set up to investigate alternative business plans will need to understand the aspirations of the Board (which may be unstated) if its proposals are to stand any chance of success (even if there are some specified hard criteria for the business plan itself).

Regardless of the type of project, we tend to see hard criteria as the exclusive basis for judging success. They are, of course, important, but they often express only minimum rather than the optimum. They may not be the basis of assessment when matters are less straightforward. Most salespeople are set very clear financial targets in terms of the volume of orders they must attain in each quarter. But the best salespeople go further, and distinguish themselves by the way they treat their clients. Achieving a sales target can hardly be called 'success' if goodwill is lost in the process.

The soft and less easily measured criteria of the project are often more important than the hard and easily-measured criteria. For example, you might be installing a computer system for a company; it works very effectively, and is delivered on time and within budget. However, if it is not user-friendly, because criteria for this were not made clear in the definition phase, the customer will not be satisfied and the project will not be a full success. It is part of the job of a project leader to 'tease out' such soft criteria in discussion with the client and end users at the start of the project.

Hard success criteria tend to relate to *what* is done. Soft success criteria relate more to *how* it is done. Figure 5.3 expresses this.

High standards in the less tangible areas associated with both products and services have become crucial to an organization's competitive edge; so soft criteria are not just 'nice to have' extras, but essential elements of success. Living up to the soft criteria will sometimes limit damage from some failure in relation to hard criteria. For instance, quick, honest information about problems or incidents can buy stakeholder tolerance of a delay. One high-tech company says: 'What can damage us most is overselling and underdelivering'; this is very much an attitude of mind. Naturally, it is still necessary to deliver good products that work to specification, but many competitors may be able to do that just as well.

For many project leaders, it is extremely important to discover what the soft criteria are. This gives them the edge over the competition. Success criteria, both hard and soft, can sometimes only be discovered by detective work. Stakeholders may not deliberately hide information about criteria; it may just be that they have not gone through the discipline of formally defining them. However, the criteria will be implicit in what they do and how they react. The project leader can help

Hard criteria (What)	Soft criteria (How)
Tangible Quantitative For example, you must meet: ● deadlines ● performance specifications ● specific quality standards ● cost requirements ● resource constraints.	Intangible Qualitative For example, you must demonstrate: ● a co-operative attitude ● a positive image ● total quality ● total project commitment ● an appreciation of the level of risk involved ● ethical conduct.

Figure 5.3 Success criteria

them to arrive at the criteria through discussion of their actions and reactions. Seeing what they *don't* want can help here.

Obvious and less obvious criteria

Figure 5.4 gives some of the criteria which need to be considered by the project leader in building up an understanding of what will represent success in the project. Operating only on the basis of the open/hard criteria declared by the stakeholders at the outset will give rise to misunderstandings and confrontations; the chances of success will be considerably reduced.

We suggest you run through your current project and ask:

● What is the expected output?
● What are the open/hard criteria?
● What are the open/soft criteria?
● Do you suspect any hard or soft criteria are hidden under the table?

Brain storming and clustering

Brain storming with a group of people is a very good way of rapidly sketching out some of the central activities and processes that might need to be undertaken in the project. A very simple way to do this is to use sticky Post-it notes. Give the group a briefing of what you know about the project so far and any thoughts that you have on it. Ask them, as you talk, to write down on Post-it notes any actions, tasks, activities or processes that they believe might need to be carried out to realize the project. These can then be stuck up on a wall or flipchart for everybody to see. You can then hold a further group brain storming process where people shout out further examples and you write these up on Post-it notes. Quantity not quality of ideas is the most important consideration at this point. People should not feel they have to be 'sensible'.

	Hard	Soft
In the open		
Declared, visible, openly discussed by all parties	– Performance specs – Time, money – Contractual terms and conditions – Delivery terms and quality.	– How project controlled – Review meetings – What procedures to be used if it goes wrong – How communication is to take place.
Under the table		
Withheld deliberately, undeclared by oversight, or not usually discussed, but very influential	– 'Real' budget constraints that are arising or foreseeable – e.g. delivery dates, resource availability	political concerns – 'don't rock the boat' or 'if anything goes wrong you're on your own' or 'don't reduce my visibility with top managers'.
May emerge		
Unknown by both parties, but should be dealt with positively when they emerge	– New options arise from practical events and experience – The unexpected enforces different constraints – 'Acts of God' – crisis	– Risks too large for the client personally – Outcomes from joint participant days of problem-solving.

Figure 5.4 The obvious and less obvious success criteria

You can then work with the group to cluster groups of Post-it notes into related activities. You can also then apply judgement to prioritize or schedule the phasing of activities. This quite rapidly gives you both a high-level plan and some elements of lower-level plans which are good enough at this stage.

Capability audits

Having seen some of the suggested activities, you are then in a better position to begin to estimate what kinds of capabilities you might require to complete the project. You can do this by yourself, but again, using a group of people makes the process more efficient and more complete, particularly if you can pull together people who have either some interest in or contribution to the project. This can be done quite rapidly.

The key question that you need to ask is: 'What will we need to be good at in order to achieve this project successfully?' You can use a number of triggers for your thinking. Obviously, the outline activity plan drawn up from the brainstorm is one. Another might be to ask yourself what skills and resources you would require, under the following headings:

- technical skills
- commercial skills
- political skills
- financial skills
- communication skills
- managerial skills
- gaining commitment
- planning skills
- contacts and networks
- securing resources.

Such an audit would rapidly enable you to see which capabilities lies within the organization, together with their likely availability, and which capabilities you will either have to develop internally or procure from elsewhere. These are your capability gaps, and filling them is frequently a time-consuming business much underestimated in planning by project managers. This is a common source of delay and slippage.

Visioning

The most significant success factor for project teams is that they have a common and shared idea of what difference they are trying to make as a result of the project. Such a vision can be built up by exploring questions with stakeholders and project team members, such as:

- How will this project make a difference to the organization?
- How would we know that this project had been highly successful?
- What in your wildest dreams would you like this project to achieve?

Translating the answers to such questions into a vision statement for the project creates a very powerful communications tool, not only for project team members, but also as a way of checking with and communicating to stakeholders and other interested parties throughout the course of the project. It also serves at a later stage to help you to keep the project on track.

Conclusion

Frequently, where there has been a skilful series of iterations in the scoping process, the project definition finally agreed is substantially different from that initially presented. This is a sign of success not failure. The project has been clarified, is more clearly linked to business needs, and has the political backing and will to ensure that it succeeds, so most of its problems are over. The implementation will, of course, have its ups and downs, but the ground has been well prepared.

A project based on the firm foundations of effective scoping, has much greater chances of survival than one which lacks this basic prerequisite. The scoping process should be both highly supportive and highly challenging. It is the basis for a project's success.

Part III
Managing the project

At last, the phase that traditional project managers think of as the real nuts and bolts project work. But even in this section on implementation we'll be suggesting that you need to pay attention not only to the tasks or activities of the project, but also to ensuring that your team and your organization remain receptive and supportive towards it right through to its conclusion.

6 The project start-up process

Once you have completed the scoping process and achieved reasonable clarity about what you are trying to achieve and commitment to it, then you and your colleagues have to change up a gear or two. Your job now is to gather the team together and to get it working effectively – fast! That is your primary objective in the project start-up process.

Taking time for reflection at the start of a project is not easy. Again and again, in training simulations, in work-based projects which form part of a development activity, and in real life projects, we discover the tendency to plunge into the project or task without taking adequate time to clarify:

- *Why* are we doing this?
- *What* are our assumptions and expectations about the project and our roles?
- *How* are we going to operate?

The often-quoted example of the difference between Western and Japanese management illustrates this point perfectly. The average time-to-market for a new model of automobile in Japan is half that in the West. The difference is accounted for by looking at how the two cultures spend that time. In Japan, they spend – to Western minds – an enormously long period discussing the project definition, testing commitment to it, scoping ways of working and interrelationships before 'doing' anything! More than half the project time is spent in this way, and the implementation phase takes up the remainder. In the West, the picture is different. Typically, implementation starts relatively early in the project life cycle. This uncovers issues not anticipated or dealt with early on, and the project cycles back into re-design/re-think, followed by another implementation phase, and so on. The overall time needed is twice as much as in Japan. The consequence is that serious implementation issues are not discovered until too late – when major review and re-planning becomes costly both in time and money. Team start-up is therefore one of the most critical phases in the project. By 'start-up' we mean the assembly of the project team, the defining of the project's success criteria (the 'What') and of the team's way of working (the 'How'). So, let us begin to look in more detail at what the important issues are in this phase.

Assembling the team

Putting the team together can be an awesome task for many project leaders, not least because it may feel as if other parts of the organization are determined to prevent you from succeeding. Assembling the team is a design job: ensuring the right mixture of people and combination of roles to best achieve the task. There are a number of factors to be considered. The first is to consider what type of people will fit your type of project.

Fitting the team to the project

There are two theories about the relationship between task, people and roles. The 'classical' theory starts with analysing the task and activities to be undertaken, and from that defines the roles that are needed. You then look for people who can best fit those roles. The alternative theory starts with the task but focuses on success criteria. It then looks for the people who would be committed and able to contribute towards fulfilling those criteria. Their roles are then evolved in line with what they can contribute.

The latter approach is more flexible and suits the needs of more open projects. Temporary and open project teams are often unclear about the roles and structures they will need. Forcing them into a traditional structure restricts individual contributions. Figures 6.1 and 6.2 summarize the main considerations in assembling the right people for different types of projects.

The politics of team selection

When you are beginning to make the case to include the people you want in your core team, you will inevitably come across custom and practice in the allocation of people. Large project-based organizations, such as oil exploration companies,

PROJECT TYPE WITHIN CONTINUUM		
Concrete/High visibility	*Temporary/High visibility*	*Open/High visibility*
1. Specialist skills known: get experts 2. Bargain high for the best 3. Roles clearly defined – overlaps and integration of expertise needed 4. Ensure a balance in ways of working and team contribution 5. Unite team early – confront problems together.	1. Skills needed may not be clear 2. Creative people needed at early phases. Change to implementers later. Flexible to outsiders 3. Rapidly changing membership 4. Attract interested, keen people 5. Unite team towards broad goals 6. Recognize and harness different team contributions.	1. Unclear what needs to happen, difficult to define skills and knowledge required. Formal rules not helpful 2. Focus on people with fire and optimism 3. Unite the team with common values on what is to be achieved 4. Define own ways of working, self selecting 5. Flexibility to outsiders.

Figure 6.1 Getting high-visibility teams off the ground

PROJECT TYPE WITHIN CONTINUUM		
Concrete/High visibility	*Temporary/Low visibility*	*Open/Low visibility*
1. Specialist skills known: role definition helpful 2. May not get the best people. Development plans may be needed to cover people gaps. Use invisible team 3. Focus on balancing the working preferences and different team contributions. 4. Focus on creating unity of purpose and insist on confronting early blockages.	1. Skills needed will emerge. Roles may not be helpful 2. Important to get going with those who are interested 3. Difficult battles with other managers over time and conflicting priorities 4. Rapidly changing membership 5. Recognize and tap into the contributions and range of abilities that exist 6. Use the visible team to fill gaps – spread the load 7. Focus on creating the unity and energy to continue. There will be disappointments.	1. Very unclear what needs to happen, low-key activity 2. Identify interested people who are trying on their own to do something similar 3. Ensuring sufficient time to achieve anything substantial will be hard 4. Loss of momentum will be a continuous question.

Figure 6.2 Getting low-visibility teams off the ground

have large pools of people, and there are managers whose role is solely that of allocating people to projects. In smaller companies with fairly concrete projects, individuals either with special talents or with the eagerness to be involved are usually in greater demand. So they go to the highest bidder.

A number of approaches to team selection are used:

- A top group of managers or a committee decide, producing a list of team members based on pragmatic criteria. The project leader may or may not be in the group and may have to guess why he/she has been allocated the individuals in the team.
- A senior manager appoints – the project leader has no choice.
- The project leader influences the selection process, putting together a team from inside the organization or by hiring new full-time recruits or specialist advisers from outside.
- The project leader and core team members select the rest of the team themselves, to make sure that the fit is optimal. This is more common with temporary or open projects.
- Where there is no clear or permanent project leader, the team can be self-selecting, or individuals may volunteer.

These approaches are viable across the project continuum; most difficulties are encountered with projects which are more open and have low visibility. The only negotiating tactic at that end is to appeal to an individual's personal interest, and foster that.

Ensuring the right mix

Whatever the political realities, the project leader will want to ensure that, no matter why they were selected, team members have the time and ability to contribute to the project. Where a degree of choice is possible, project leaders should consider the following criteria for selecting team members. (Where no choice is possible, they can be used to assess the team/skills mix.)

- Who is interested in this project?
- Who is keen to contribute and believes the project is important and desirable?
- Who has special technical skills/expertise/experience that are needed?
- Who can represent important interest groups (clients, end users)?
- Who will 'fit' with the way we want to work?
- Who has organization clout/credibility/connections to help the project?
- Who represents/understands the 'antis'/the opposition?
- Who would benefit through self-development or corporate exposure from being associated with this project?
- Who has external networks that might be useful to the project?
- Who has special non-technical skills (i.e. communication, political access, etc.)?

Accelerating team development

Once you have assembled your team, the toughest part of project start-up is behind you. But there is more to do.

We know of project teams that launch their projects by gathering the visible and invisible teams together to outline the Big Picture. Perhaps more important is the opportunity for members of the team to put names to faces and to start building the identity of the team. One large contractor working in the Far East found that a banquet which should have been held to celebrate completion of the work had been organized to take place before the job had started. The mistake turned out to be the single most useful event in the early stage of the project. Communicating with people in the team was much easier after the banquet. A similar example is the branch of a political party whose election team used a combination of headquarters and local officials to paint and clean the venues, such as church halls, before campaigning started.

Organize something together – preferably informal and not too project-orientated – so that people can get to know each other in a relaxed way.

The rationale

However, this will not be enough, but it will be a good start, for high-quality teamwork does not come naturally. The team needs to understand in more detail what impact it should be making. Individuals come with their own agendas, pressures and limitations. Few will share a concept of what skills a high-performing team needs; individuals will bring elements, but not the whole. And even skilled teamworkers, when they come together, have to go through the normal team development stages of 'forming', 'storming' and 'norming' before they can really start 'performing'. Your job is to accelerate their progress through these stages, to do this by finding out the most appropriate ways to work together using the full resources that the team members bring, and to make this happen rapidly. And this, paradoxically, takes time – an investment that will repay you handsomely in terms of much-reduced wasted time, effort and slippage at later stages.

Whom do I involve?

Obviously, your core team members will be the main project drivers and are the ones who need to be involved in project start-up activities, workshops or conferences. There is no simple rule. Just ask yourself: 'Who would benefit by being involved?' We have run start-up workshops for project teams involving between six and sixty people!

The invisible team link

Like temporary or open project team members, all invisible team members have other demands on their time. The task of the project leader and core team members is to make it as easy as possible for invisible team members to come into the team at the appropriate time and contribute of their best. There is no inherent reason why the invisible team should be committed to the project. Their commitment and motivation have to be *earned* by the visible team members, who must demonstrate that they appreciate their situations. Negotiate the nature and extent of the contribution each invisible team member is to make so that your expectations of each other are compatible.

Near the time of their actual involvement, invite them to meetings and brief them extensively on the Big Picture, how the team works and its operating ground rules. It is just as important as for visible team members that they understand how their role fits with everyone else's and that they see some of the benefits for themselves. Give them as much notice as possible so that they can plan their commitment to the project team around their other responsibilities.

It is common to devise a system of 'counterparts' in which every invisible team member has a contact person in the visible team to whom they can relate and who is responsible for keeping them in touch with everything that is happening. We have seen this system used to great effect in a complex shipbuilding project involving very many different contractors. The object is to build 'credits' with invisible team members. In this way, 'outsiders' become 'insiders'; enemies become friends and supporters. The strategy is one of involvement, not exclusion. The high-performing project team works hard to break down any barriers between themselves and external stakeholders. They take note of the outsider's perception of the team, and work hard to ensure that it is seen in a positive light both within and outside the organization. This is the essence of collaborative working.

You can extend this to bringing members of your client's organization into your project team. We know of several project teams working on large projects where the client has representatives sitting in the same offices as the project team members. In one oil exploration project, the contractors have moved most of their people into the client's offices. In this way, the team is dramatically re-defined.

Project start-up – A team development agenda

In the early stages of start-up, you should set yourself four objectives:

- to create some sense of team identity
- to begin to discuss and share perceptions of the overall team purpose and success criteria
- to begin to answer for each team member the question 'What's in it for me?'
- to draw out the underlying concerns that individuals have about the project or the team or any other issues that might make them hold back their commitment.

The rest of this chapter will give you some specific ideas and tools for achieving these objectives.

Involving the core team members in the planning process is not only a recipe for more effective and realistic planning, it is also the major mechanism that you have at your disposal for welding the team together rapidly into an effective unit.

The question is: what sort of agenda do you need to have for this planning process? We have developed a structure for working on these issues based on a previous book *Superteams: Building Organisational Success Through High Performing Teams* (1986, HarperCollins). We divide it into two broad categories: 'Planning the What' – paying attention to defining the more tangible task, content or timing related issues – and 'Planning the How' – developing and agreeing ground rules and processes which describe the functioning of the team and the more intangible enablers to ensure its effectiveness.

Planning the 'What'

Success criteria

What are the success criteria for the project – the critical indices against which the teams success will be judged? The team will need to understand both the stated purpose of the project as seen by key stakeholders (e.g. sponsor, client, project leader), and also the unstated purpose. Purposes may be unstated because they are politically unacceptable, because they are not really thought through, or because they are not readily quantifiable. They will also need to appreciate whether there is conflict between stakeholders, and what, if anything, can be done about it. (Success criteria are covered in more depth in Chapter 5, pp. 85–7.)

Who does what, when?

Prior to your team development event you should ask each of your core team members to work up draft plans, at an agreed level of detail. These can then be presented to the whole group. Sub-groups can then split up to look for possible clashes, possible interface problems and ways of cutting out wasted time, and also suggesting intermediate milestones: highly visible points at which progress and achievement can be marked out along the way. In this way, many good ideas come up and the team as a whole comes to feel that it owns and understands the plan and how it all fits together. Through this collective planning process they all have the necessary overview and commitment to be able to act more responsibly as the plan unfolds. Ignorance, on the other hand, breeds indifference.

Selecting the right planning tools

Traditional project management grew up around the development of sophisticated computer-based estimating and planning tools. These have been invaluable in large-scale projects, but can be too complex and specialist for most organizational projects. (See more detailed discussion of software tools in Chapter 8, pp. 123–4.)

Given our strong belief that planning should involve all core team members, what simple tools and techniques seem to work?

- *Plan backwards not forwards* This may sound perverse but it produces good results. Get the team to focus on the *end results* that you are trying to achieve. This should be clear if you have done your scoping well. Then get the team to work backwards, thinking of everything that would have to be done to achieve that goal.
- *Brainstorming* In trying to imagine all the possible tasks and activities you will need to carry out, start off with no particular structure, inviting members to shout out their ideas. These should be recorded either on flipcharts, or even better on large Post-it notes which can then easily be categorized and sorted into an outline schedule.
- *Work breakdown structure* You can also sort the Post-it notes into different levels of detail. High-level activities or clusters (for example, 'internal communications') can be broken down into lower-level categories (such as

'workshops', 'newsletter', 'informal briefings') and so on into even more detail.

- *Bar charts* Sometimes known as Gantt Charts (see Figure 8.1), these are a very simple way of showing the essential high-level activities in a project visually, so that the whole team can quickly understand how the different parts are related.

  In a more complex project, you can send a sub-section of your team away to work up more detailed plans on one of the 'bars' (as in our example above about 'internal communications'). They can then come back and summarize their work with another (lower-level) bar chart.

- *Dependencies* Many tasks can be undertaken in parallel, and you should strive for this for speed's sake where possible. But some tasks cannot start until others have been completed. You and team members should be very clear about these linkages. Failure to spot them will cause you many problems later.

Ensuring plans are realistic

Whichever tools you use, it is your job as project leader to take steps to ensure that the plans that emerge are realistic. One of the major sources of slippage in projects is that the initial plans were based on poor analysis of what needed to be done and/or naive estimates of how long different stages would take. Project leaders also frequently feel under pressure to deliver. In the worst cases their sponsors or clients have already committed themselves to completion dates without consultation. It takes a tough project leader to challenge this *fait accompli*. It is often tempting to go along with it and just pray! But where the stakes are high, no self-respecting project leaders should allow themselves to be set up for failure in this way. Good scoping should have already confronted this issue. But equally, good-quality, credible plans and estimates are powerful data with which to argue for more realistic timescales or a compromise in the scope or success criteria, or more resources.

So what can you do to check that your plans are realistic? First, you can ensure that the people who will actually carry out the work draw up the estimates. You need to have discussed the ground rules for estimating beforehand so that people don't play games of overestimating to give themselves contingency time, which delays the whole project. Second, you can consult others with previous experience in some aspects of your project. Third, you can ensure that team members build up their time estimates from the detailed list of tasks in the work breakdown structure which the team has developed. This makes the estimating process more structured and precise. Do not accept the back-of-envelopes approach from your team members. Fourth, you need to be very aware of the types of tasks that are somehow never considered in the planning process, and are simply left out. Some of these are vital tasks which are time-consuming but intangible, many of them to do with managing the 'How' of the project rather than the 'What' (see below). The most common invisible time-stealers that are frequently ignored in plans are:

- communication processes – e.g. the process of informing people, helping them to understand, updating them and getting feedback, and reviewing
- key decision milestones outside your control – e.g. gaining approval for a primary project element at a Board Meeting or a particular committee. If you miss a specific meeting, there is often not another one for months, and you may have to devote a great deal of time to seeking approval individually from committee members
- team members representing other functions or external agencies who constantly have to refer elsewhere for decisions
- the difficulty of organizing meetings involving several busy people
- the need for end users to be brought up to date and perhaps trained where necessary in using its outputs
- selling ideas and warming up key decision-makers in advance so that they have all the information necessary to understand what you are asking of them
- assembling all the resources your team might need – often relatively insignificant matters like installing a special telephone or fax line or a new PC seem to take inordinately long because of cumbersome company procedures.

Finally, when the plan is almost finalized, you should bring the core team together for a session where you encourage everyone to think of ways in which you could do things more efficiently. Is there duplication, for instance? Could more be done earlier, or in parallel, to save time? Are there short cuts that could be taken that would not compromise quality? These types of questions should not only be asked now, but continuously throughout the project.

Planning the 'How'

Your objective under this heading is to begin to discuss 'the way we need to do things round here' in order to be successful. You'll be starting discussion about the norms, and ground rules and processes that are vital. Discussions of these 'soft' issues is not always easy and does not come naturally, especially to technical specialists. But we know that the 'How' factor is *the* difference between failure and success. Planning the 'What' is more comfortable. It is the easy stage – it's necessary, but unfortunately, not sufficient in itself. So you have to be patient and allow your team members to learn this new language slowly and focus their attention. Elements of this new 'process' language should include:

- *How will we manage the outside?* – How will we position and market the project in our organization? Who are our friends and enemies? What help/resources do we need from outside the team? What help and resources do we need that we don't have in the core team?

- *Leadership and membership* – What do we expect of the team leader: e.g. providing the Big Picture, keeping the team on track, marketing the project? What do we expect of team members: e.g. taking responsibility, fulfilling commitments, keeping others informed? Who will provide drive and energy? Who will be keeping us on track? Does the project leader have to provide all the leadership? What are the different ways members can contribute? Are we aware of all our collective skills and experience? Which are delegated responsibilities and which ones should be shared collectively?

- *The team apart* – How will we stay in touch between meetings? How will we deal with competing priorities: the project and our other commitments? Do we follow through and do what we say we will between meetings? How will we keep information flowing? What systems and technologies can help?

- *The team together* – How will we manage our meetings productively, and ensure they re-energize us, not drain us? What style and format will suit our personal preferences and the project needs? How often will we meet? How will we manage conflicting views/priorities/style? (All project teams experience conflicts! The skilled ones understand that these are an important source of testing, understanding and generating ideas.)

How not to start up a project

A head office division within a large retail company had recently been restructured. The restructuring had resulted in new roles for the top team (most of whom had not been involved in planning it). Two new members of the team were hired from outside the company. This top team were given the project of implementing the restructuring. Six months on, things were not going well. Morale was low in several areas. The division had twice failed to deliver to its customers on key tasks. Previously harmonious relationships among the top team were showing cracks. The division's performance had been questioned at Board level. There was suspicion between the 'old guard' and the newcomers. As time progressed and views became polarized it became harder for the top team to address these matters.

Success criteria

The project team had not clearly defined the project's success criteria. The broad statement 'implementing the reorganization' had been used, without a clear definition of performance measures, what key clients expected, what important outputs needed to run smoothly, what management style was appropriate and what new ways of working were required. The team overestimated the level of understanding and commitment of vital stakeholders, leaving them confused about why the changes had happened and what the aims of the new division were.

Managing sponsors

The project team did not have a robust understanding of the sponsor – the Divisional Director. She was moving towards retirement and was starting to disengage herself from involvement with the division. They felt frustrated because she failed to get Board commitment to requests for staff and resources for key projects.

The team together

The team continued their monthly business review meetings, which did not provide an adequate forum to address important issues such as:

- How do our new roles interrelate and what difference do we expect of each other?
- What are our long-term goals?
- How are we supporting the two newcomers? (The newcomers had very different styles to the existing team. This quickly became a source of friction on both sides, but was never dealt with.)

Managing the outside

Major customers saw the reorganization as a source of irritation and interruption, and were not sold the potential benefits to them.

The team apart

The team was geographically dispersed, and met only monthly. Despite good intentions, follow-through on agreed issues was patchy. There had also been a major delay in connecting all team members to the electronic mail system, which caused further frustrations and problems.

Conclusion

In the first stages of a project there is much uncertainty: about its purpose, about the other team members, whether it will be enjoyable, and so on. The team is like a great iceberg – only a small part of it is visible. To overcome some of this uncertainty should be your main aim when the team first comes together.

'I'm not interested in politics. I just want to get on with the job.' This is a frequent but unrealistic cry from project leaders. Team selection is political;

reactions have to be weighed and compromises made to ensure the right mix of people. Teamworking is also a development experience. The team that you start with is not the one you finish with, even if it comprises the same members.

Team start-up is an opportunity to build solid foundations, so that cracks don't appear in the project later on. The team need to pay attention to themselves:

- their skills/strengths/personal motivations and expectations of each other
- their understanding of what the project is said to be about, and what it is actually about
- how they are going to work together – ground rules
- what they are going to do – the project scoping and plan
- how they will manage key interfaces/stakeholders.

Time spent early on in addressing these issues will reap significant benefits as the project unfolds.

Three further team start-up exercises

Exercise 1: Accelerating team development – The early stages

At the early stages of team formation, much useful information lies hidden, iceberg-like, below the surface. Reactions, thoughts and feelings about the team stay private as new members test the water to see if it's safe. There's a lot of uncertainty about.

Here are some clues to some of the things that may be going on beneath the surface. Helping these issues to surface, by gently probing or by revealing your own thoughts and feelings, can often provide a starting point for team development:

- How clear are members about what might be demanded of them (by sponsor, client, leader)?
- What might be the different attitudes and feelings (positive and negative) that new group members bring?
- What different aspirations and success criteria might people from different backgrounds and functions bring?
- Where do members' loyalties and commitment lie – to the task force, to their department, elsewhere?
- What's in it for the project team members?
- How clear are individuals about their roles, responsibilities and working relationships?
- Are members part of the team because of:
  - their appropriate knowledge and skills
  - their position or status

- being told to join
- not being wanted elsewhere?
- To what extent are other roles or commitments competing for their time?
- What history and past experience do individuals bring with them that may help or hinder their attitude to this team?
- What action must be taken, by whom, to resolve any such issues that are likely to have an adverse effect on team or individual performance?

Exercise 2: Accelerating team development – Understanding the project in its context

Ask team members to write down their answers to the following questions individually. Then structure a discussion where they reveal their answers. Ensure that it's all recorded for subsequent use.

- *Purpose*
  - What is the *stated* purpose of the project as described by the project leader, sponsor, client, team members, others?
  - What is the *unstated* purpose of the project as seen by the same stakeholders?
- *Consequences*
  - What are the *intended* consequences of the project (both in hard and soft criteria terms)?
  - What might be some of the *unintended* consequences (positive and negative)?
  - How could we reduce or reverse the negative consequences?
- *Vision/potential*
  - What, in our wildest dreams, *could* we achieve if we really pulled all the stops out and carried everyone along with us?

Exercise 3: Accelerating team development – role clarification

Identify the differences in these perceptions, and ensure they are resolved:

- *Team leader to team member*
  - This is what I see you actually doing currently in your role.
  - This is what I think you ought to be doing in your role.
- *Team member to team leader*
  - This is what I see myself actually doing in my role.
  - This is what I think I ought to be doing in my role.
- *Team leader to team member (and vice versa)*
  - How am I preventing you being as effective as you might be?
  - Here's what I think I can do to help you in your role.
  - In what other ways would you like me to help you in your role?

7 'Marketing' to the stakeholders

We *must* communicate with people involved in the project. Every project leader knows this truth, and many quake at the thought. How to fit the time to communicate into a tight project plan? There are so many things to do. Which members of the team can communicate well? Who will do more harm than good? How to persuade busy users, managers, suppliers and customers to listen? What to do with unwelcome objections and comments? Does communication make a difference anyway? This is a sample of the ideas that cross a project leader's mind.

By adapting some of the ideas and tools of marketing, you can integrate communication activities into the project plans as legitimate work packages, with time, people and money allocated to them. Communicating is then part of the project right from the start. Stakeholders are built into the project, thereby accelerating effective implementation and rendering it is seamless, rather than all the lurking difficulties emerging at project handover, leading, in the worst case, to rejection. Communication is particularly relevant to open projects, for example in information technology, where the success of the technology depends on how well it is adopted by the end users and how willingly it is integrated into their work. In order to achieve this level of acceptance, communication – or as we'll call it, 'marketing' – cannot be random or an afterthought. It is vital to the project's success, so it must involve a programme of planned, integrated activities that aim to build robust, long-term relationships.

What does marketing offer?

Surely marketing is just about persuading people to buy cans of beans or washing powder? Well, yes in part, but have you heard of 'buyer's remorse'? If you have been persuaded to buy something against your better judgement, then you rarely re-purchase, and you frequently tell your friends your frank opinion of the people who cheated you. Marketing is concerned with building loyalty to a product or service, where the customer willingly and automatically buys again.

Marketing ideas relevant to projects

Awareness-building

When introducing new products, there is a need to create awareness of:

- its existence
- its purpose
- the benefits
- what it looks like and how it works.

Unless we know of a product's existence, we cannot decide whether we want it or not. A market is created by informing potential buyers. Today we are well aware of toothpaste and what it does for us: how it protects our teeth and makes us attractive to be with. But just imagine the task that faced the early toothpaste manufacturers! The market had to be created through publicizing information and establishing credible benefits.

Market segmentation

In the field of consumer products, we are well aware that different people drive different cars, depending on how much they can afford, how they want to look (is their image fast and racy, or sedate?) and what else they think is important – should the car be safe and environmentally friendly, or high-performing and technically advanced?

From their needs and views of themselves, individuals will have different profiles of interests and concerns. They will buy in different ways, therefore marketing will need to take account of this. Once buyers have willingly purchased, they want to be satisfied, and if the product meets their expectations they can easily be persuaded to buy from the same source again. Brand loyalty is built up.

Marketing people therefore segment their market carefully, identifying what is important to each group. For each market segment they build a profile of the perceived benefits, their way of life and their values. They design their communication to fit this profile. Advertisements will only appear in selected places, the message will be angled accordingly, and the expectations will be accurately set. When they get it right, buying is easy, there is little resistance, and the good reputation of their product or service is established.

Relationship-building

In the field of services, we are more concerned with continuing expectations that are tested out daily through experience of what happens. The relationship is dynamic: we remember most clearly those incidents where something untoward happens, for example when the garage did not set the timing of the car's engine effectively, or the invoice was incorrect, or the mechanic on the phone was rude.

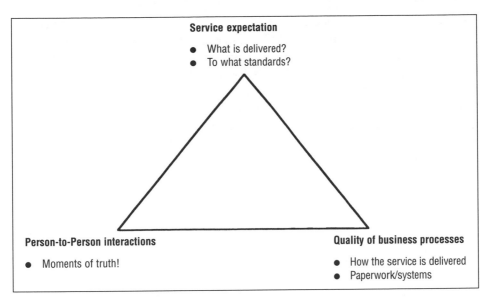

Figure 7.1 Elements of a service relationship

Services involve establishing and maintaining a relationship that has mutual advantages and is interdependent. This relies, in broad terms, on three elements (see Figure 7.1).

Clearly, if the basics in terms of service delivery do not exist, we become very disenchanted, but if the other two elements are strong, then we are more likely to be positively disposed. So, if I can call the garage and a friendly person, in whom I have confidence, fixes my problem quickly, I will be forgiving. This is what Jan Carlson of SAS called the 'moment of truth'! If no constructive action is forthcoming, I will be more assertive, or even aggressive or obstructive, and will look elsewhere. However, a relationship does not simply involve being friendly, it is like an equation of different elements that interact with each other and need to be constantly balanced.

Marketing plan

If we watch television or read Sunday newspapers, we cannot help noticing how frequently marketeers remind us of their products and services. They know that we have many other matters on our minds and will not have their product in focus, even if we are favourably disposed towards it. Repetition and familiarity are important in keeping our attention. So marketing is carefully planned to ensure that the appropriate message is directed to each market segment, and that this message is repeated frequently.

Feedback Marketing plans are not complete without feedback. New information is fed into further marketing initiatives, and incorporates the buyer's reactions. Modification of all aspects of the relationship is important, otherwise how do you know if what you *think* customers are interested in is in fact what they want? Customers can generally react to specific situations and tell you what their priorities are. An automobile company spent many millions on reducing the number of warranty claims, which were causing concern to customers. However, what most worried the customers was not the claims themselves but the inconvenience of being without a car while theirs was being repaired. The automobile manufacturer needed to pay attention to providing temporary transport, as well as reducing warranty claims.

Steps in a marketing plan

Through market research:

- segment the market
- construct profiles
- identify benefits and objections
- prepare focused communication to appeal to each segment
- try out selected communications – obtain feedback
- implement plans – wider segments
- test the product – carry out trials
- collect reactions and feedback.

Review and re-plan:

- analyse feedback
- re-plan to take account of customer reactions.

There may be several cycles of this plan, linked to the success of the product.

Project leaders and marketing

Who is the customer?

It helps if we think of end users, suppliers, contractors and other stakeholders as customers. What is the difference? It is a question of attitude. For instance, users are a passive breed who have to take what they are given. They are a faceless, anonymous lot who are at the end of a chain of complex tasks. They should be grateful for what they get. Customers, on the other hand, have a choice – they are individuals who need to be encouraged to buy. They can be seen as purchasers who should want to continue to support a product or a service. They are worthy of continuous effort, thought and planning – they are certainly not an afterthought.

Internal colleagues as customers?

Many people experience difficulties in seeing people who are fellow employees within the same organization as customers, mainly because there is no choice – 'You will have this system', 'This is the building or floor you will work on', 'These are the policies and procedures that will be implemented.' Often this is true, choice *is* limited. But what may be unlimited is the willingness and enthusiasm of people in taking on something new, implementing it and using it to its full capacity. As they say: 'You can take a horse to water but you can't make it drink.' So the question is how to make people positively want and welcome what you are providing.

Communication and missed opportunities

Fellow employees are accustomed to standard communications in the organization's style. This leads to a generalized communication, either written or personally presented, that aims to cover everybody's interests, frequently missing what makes sense to most people, and overwhelming many along the way. Internal customers are not 'real' customers, so they do not need to be targeted with specially-designed and frequent communication. This is seen as wasting valuable time and money on internal people. However, so frequently we hear disappointed project leaders and their managers saying: 'I don't understand why they are so resistant and can't see the benefits.'

Creating willing participation

What can you do in the early stages of the project to create willing involvement? The basic question is 'How can I run this project with the key stakeholders in mind?'

From stakeholder mapping to market segmentation

Chapter 5 on scoping encourages you to map your stakeholders and understand their interests. In terms of the service relationship, you will have ideas about their service expectations in terms of deliverables and benefits. The other elements of the service relationship concern how they will need to be involved with the project as it progresses, plus what 'moments of truth' will occur to lead the particular stakeholder to believe that the project's activity has them in mind.

An example of this approach being used successfully involved a large telecommunications company's logistics department. At any one time they had eighty different projects in progress, each being managed with a variety of sophisticated and basic project planning approaches. Senior management realized that for very critical projects there were interdependencies that were hard to spot, and harder to manage flexibly. Attention had been given to standardizing approaches, but these had not been well received by the project leaders and their teams. The project leader for the 'Software Migration Project' inherited a predetermined software package, an established business case and an unwilling set of stakeholders who had to be persuaded to convert to a new set of automated procedures.

The project leader decided that the stakeholders could be segmented into four groups:

- *senior management*, who wanted
  - to track dependencies and shift resources
  - easy-to-read, graphical summary data
- *experienced project managers*, who wanted
  - to retain control of their projects
  - to use the existing hardware
  - to transfer the data from the existing software into the new system
- *inexperienced project managers*, who wanted
  - to know how much extra time it would take them to learn new planning techniques, and how to operate the software
  - to know what training and back-up support would be available
- *programme office technical support*, who wanted
  - to be sure that the software was reliable
  - to be able to produce quality senior management reports.

From this analysis the project leader decided to hold separate introductory presentations for all the different groups, with questions and discussions aimed at addressing the underlying worries. She conducted a campaign using a logo, posters, newsletter updates, short exhibitions and briefing meetings that had to be attended at lunch-time or in the early evening. She ensured that the training materials were documented early, and announced a marketing plan that enabled people to understand how they would be trained before the system went live. The training was targeted specifically at each segment, it was not a standard course. There was a great deal of one-to-one coaching and on-line support. Particular attention was paid to the difficult problem of transferring the experienced project manager's data into the format acceptable to the new system. Together with the people most affected, she worked out how this would be achieved and carried out tests to determine what was involved, working with them until the new system was operating with the existing data.

Prototypes or drafts were used frequently to establish what the system could do and how information should be presented. Feedback was taken and the system modified to reflect the various stakeholders' working needs. There was a planned series of formal, and even more important, informal marketing activities.

So far, the system is being implemented and many people are voluntarily signing up for training, which is filled to capacity. This is unusual. The new software is gaining wide support as most project managers begin to see that they do not lose, and in fact may gain from being part of the migration. Difficult

Who?	Market segment
What?	Matters to this segment?
	• Deliverables
	• How/when to involve
	• What relationships are important?
Why?	What information or features are needed?
	• Test reactions/commitment
How?	Which method of communication?
	• Formal/Informal
	• Written/Face-to-face/Interactive
When?	How often? Which points in life cycle?

Figure 7.2 Elements of an internal marketing plan

problems have been jointly resolved. No rash promises have been made, but the expectations that *have* been set have been met. The customers are willing to 'buy' because internal marketing has married the people with the benefits. The project leader has been seen to concentrate on aspects that are important to the customers to make sure that these work before problems arise.

Putting together an internal marketing plan

The questions for which you need answers are set out in Figure 7.2. Working down this checklist for each segment of stakeholders in your project will suggest a number of activities and their time sequencing. Without doubt this is much more than you had ever imagined, which illustrates that internal marketing is probably 10–25% of the total project activity. In many projects, internal marketing is not planned beyond a launch or start-up activity, so naturally the pressure of time takes over and these rather important tasks are neglected.

The medium is the message

As part of the marketing plan, the project leader has to decide which marketing media to use. Formal methods such as written documents, newsletters, videos and activity reports come readily to mind. These are most useful for propagating awareness. If the Chief Executive talks about the opening of a new laboratory facility on video or even in person, then most people would understand that it is something worth his consideration. But it is unlikely that anyone with no special interest will remember more than 5% of the content one day later. That 5% will tend to be the joke he cracked or the tie he wore! If you want to build willingness

113

• Hearing	Receiving and sifting information – verbal and non-verbal
• Understanding	Making sense in terms of how I see the world
• Acting	What does this mean? What do I need to do in my context? How do I do it? Trying something out.

Figure 7.3 Steps in communication

and interest you have to engage people personally, so interactive approaches are needed, such as workshops that include presentations. However, even more necessary is the opportunity to discuss, ask questions, test reactions and think of implications. This is best provided in a facilitated workshop which is designed to include group work and feedback sessions to build and test understanding (see Figure 7.3).

Presentations give people the opportunity to hear, and if there is a large audience, it is symbolically significant that everybody has heard the same message at the same time. Interactive workshops are good at building understanding. If they are based on testing ideas, exploring prototypes, reviewing mock-ups or giving inputs to a design, they reinforce the project's direction or give stakeholders the chance to hear the trade-offs that have to be made, making it possible to solve problems while building commitment. In order to develop a sense of ownership of something and feel that they can use it, people need to engage with the meaning of the ideas and their implications. A series of short workshops is more effective than one on its own in establishing an open working method, which is particularly necessary in the case of an open project, where there are many viable options.

Training, particularly when it is designed to replicate the working environment, gives people the chance to practise gradually what they need to do, so that they become confident in the new situation. Classroom training is rarely more than an informal beginning to on-the-job coaching; support and monitoring embed new skills and behaviours. If the project involves new working practices, attitudes and behaviours, then this on-the-job support is vital at all levels in the organization. So telling people to be enthusiastically committed or to be empowered, if your project is a cultural change project, does not empower them at all. Once made aware of a project's benefit to them, they need regular personal and interactive contact with the project's outputs to be able to change their ways of working and realize the intended benefits.

Informal marketing or networking

The team as well as the project leader are marketing informally every moment of the day. Collectively, in what they do and how they do it, they create the image that the project presents to the outside world. How stakeholders experience their 'moments of truth' relates directly with how they rate the project. This may be unfair, but unfortunately that is how it is, so informal marketing is going on whether you plan it or not. The team's image can be managed actively, and informal marketing or networking can be harnessed to your advantage if you do it consciously.

Team image and culture

One of the decisions the project leader takes during the start-up phase is: 'What sort of team culture is necessary for the project?' How do you communicate with each other and stakeholders? Are you assertive? Do you only let problems emerge so that the guilty can be hunted and blamed? Are you available and easily contactable? Do you respond to telephone calls, or do you hope they will go away?

In your marketing plan, you can design the image you want to present and you can plan what you need to do to realize that image. Unfortunately, having plans is not enough. You must also establish behavioural ground rules, such as how quickly do you respond to new requests, or do you remember to pass on telephone messages if the team members answer each other's telephones? To complete the loop you need to monitor whether those behavioural standards are met, and how they are perceived by stakeholders.

Networking or informal contacts

Despite our everyday experience of organizational life, we believe that formal communications are official and therefore most important. Whilst formal communications have some validity, they are heavily supported by informal contact. We tend to take more notice of informal communication, because it is *personal* – directly with us, we are engaged in it and can respond directly to what is said and who has said it. It is alive and immediate. Spending time and energy building support informally and flushing out what is often labelled as 'resistance' is a hidden part of internal marketing. Figure 7.4 sets out a variety of activities that belong under the label 'networking'.

These roles concern energy, which means gaining organizational attention, movement and building critical mass for the project and the organizational issues that it raises:

- *Animateur* – attracts and radiates energy by talking informally to a wide range of people about the vision, the potential business impact
- *Integrator* – radiates and transfers energy by connecting together different points of view, representing the balances and dilemmas that have to be resolved, often putting the right people in touch with each other at the right moment

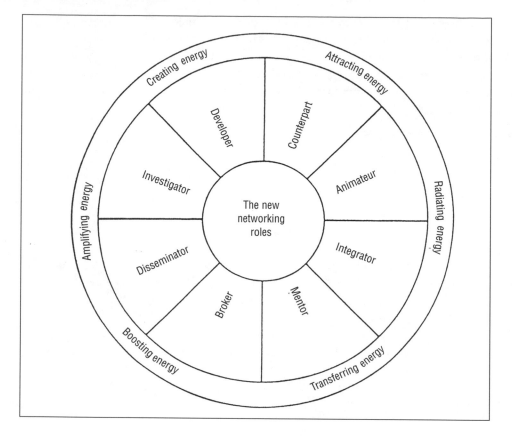

Figure 7.4 New networking roles

- *Mentor* – transfers energy by tuning market segments into the project culture, usually making explicit how the project culture works, why, and what the ground rules are in practice
- *Broker* – boosts everything by using his/her own and other people's networks, running meetings or workshops that demonstrably put stakeholders in touch with each other so that they can exchange know-how and understand differences
- *Disseminator* – amplifies energy by being the communications centre or anchor, knowing what is happening and willingly and regularly letting others know; the spider in the web: he/she 'thinks' communications
- *Investigator* – amplifies energy by being curious and excited by what others are doing or thinking, acting as a detective who is aware of resources, know-how and experience in non-traditional places
- *Developer* – creates energy in others by being good at coaching, giving positive feedback, facilitating learning between people, designing workshops, giving advice or ideas on how to transfer skills and expertise
- *Counterpart* – attracts energy by being specifically linked to another

116

stakeholder, so a team member may be the link person who works with and maintains the relationship within a market segment

Internal marketing needs to be energized, so how can you use some of these ideas to continuously stimulate the informal network around your project? You cannot do it all alone, so who is good at what in your team? Do they see internal marketing as part of their job as a team member?

Conclusion

'Communication' is an overused word. Project leaders know that they ought to do it, but often it is a side-show. Marketing is a legitimate activity that encourages customers to buy a product and continue to do so, or to engage in a service that leads to frequent contact. So building a long-term relationship is the crux of marketing. Marketeers can help project leaders to make communication more useful as an integral part of the project. Market segmentation, market planning, market testing and feedback are useful concepts. Not all marketing is formal and glossy – much involves informal networking. Networks do not just happen – they need to be created and managed so that they too are part of the internal marketing of a project.

8   Keeping on track

You've prepared the plan, your team is up and running, and you've ensured that all your stakeholders are being kept in the picture. In other words, you are now in the thick of the implementation phase of your project, the straightforward putting into practice of the plans you have drawn up. Unfortunately, as all experienced project leaders know, it doesn't work quite like that. As Henry Mintzberg, the management guru, once memorably observed: 'The real world keeps getting in the way of my plans!'

In practice, of course, we all know that the implementation phase is fraught with difficulties, and there is a danger that the project leader's role becomes one of firefighting to cope with the latest crisis rather than the provision of far-sighted guidance.

We've entitled this chapter 'Keeping on track'. Whilst the track may be fairly clear for concrete projects, it is often indistinct for open ones, but all types of projects need to be kept moving, and the same basic principles can be applied to them all.

In order to keep your project moving forward on track you need to ensure:

- that you and your team are acutely aware of insidious and unanticipated ways in which slippage can occur
- that you use appropriate monitoring tools and processes to provide rapid feedback on how the task is progressing
- that you provide regular opportunities for the team not only to review progress, but even more important, to anticipate problems over the horizon.

Beware the hidden sources of slippage

Alarm bells ring in project leaders' offices at the very mention of the word 'slippage'. The project leader's most fundamental source of satisfaction lies in bringing a project to completion on time. 'On time', of course, means that estimated completion and actual completion are identical. 'Slippage', consequently,

119

tends to be defined as an activity taking longer than was estimated. However, recent research we have carried out into sources of poor project performance in companies highlights that there are a number of other sources of slippage which do not occur directly as a result of overruns against estimates for activities in the project plan. We found these were particularly prevalent where organizations are using projects in many different ways within their business, and they have an insidious way of seriously derailing projects.

One such company is a food manufacturer, organized historically very much on production line principles. However, the need to introduce much greater variety into its range of products and to change its range of products more rapidly led it to use organizational projects to handle new product development, product launches, introduction of changes responding to new hygiene legislation and the introduction of a new manufacturing and information technology system to create much more flexible production capacity. The Board had also started forming project task forces to explore and implement different aspects of strategy such as acquisition targets and starting up Continental subsidiaries.

Because its business had moved from being relatively stable, with long production runs, to a constantly changing kaleidoscope of product developments and launches, and rapid responses to competitor activity, the number of organizational projects, to quote one of the directors, 'grew like Topsy'. These projects were initiated in many different parts of the organization. In fact, at one stage, one manager observed: 'All our work is now becoming a project.' Warning bells started sounding in the Managing Director's ears after he was asked to talk at a course being run for people who were leading such projects. Whereas he had always assumed that leading such projects was a great source of job satisfaction, the group of project leaders certainly didn't share this view. If anything, they were deeply frustrated by the organization's handling of projects. The more he probed, the more he realized that there were many different sources of under performance across these different projects which, added together, were costing his organization large sums of money in inefficient uses of resources, missing vital deadlines and the introduction of stress, conflict and low morale amongst key people.

So what 'invisible' sources of poor performance have come to light?

Dumping

Project leaders, and especially some of those perceived as the more successful, complain that their managers and other instigators allocate projects to them but take no account of their existing project and line management workload. This is particularly acute where organizations have de-layered and cut back on staff to the bone. Very few of the project leaders feel that they are allowed to say that they are overworked or to question the validity of the project, for fear that their careers and employment prospects might suffer. The way they handle this issue is simply to make their own decisions (frequently in sublime ignorance of many wider business or strategic considerations) over which projects they will put on the back burner, or alternatively, in which aspects of the different projects they will compromise on quality by taking short cuts. In several cases, project leaders had simply let projects quietly die and sink into oblivion. The frightening fact was that nobody seemed to notice!

Organizational naivety

Many of the people running projects were functional specialists of one kind or another – for example, from production, engineering or marketing departments. Many of them were relatively young and inexperienced in managerial terms, but also had very little idea of how the rest of the organization worked and of how and where important decisions were made. This naivety about some of the realities of organizational life caused them to ignore some very simple organizational considerations in their estimates and plans.

First, they all underestimated the time it would take to assemble a team of people to carry out their project. In one case, a project leader told us that she had assumed she would be given a group of people and that she would have the team up and running within a week. She discovered that it didn't work that way. She had to go out and find, persuade and generally cajole people to come to work on her project. It actually took her three months to call the first meeting.

Second, all the project leaders acknowledged they had made no allowance for what was involved in obtaining decisions either from the various departments or, on several occasions, from the Board itself. None of them had anticipated the amount of lobbying, information-giving, influencing and general preparing of the ground that would be needed to bring other people to the point of making decisions. Many assumed that a memo outlining what was required would be responded to within days by a simple 'yes'. Many of them also did not understand that crucial decisions were made at particular points, such as regular monthly Departmental or Board Meetings. Frequently, they failed to realize that information and agendas for these meetings were sometimes circulated two weeks before the meeting, and if you missed this particular point (and didn't personally approach the secretary who compiled the agenda!) you could very easily miss the boat.

The third source of naivety lay in the fact that they had never really had to juggle people's diaries and competing priorities in their previous functional roles. They were astonished by how long it took simply to gather a particular group of people together in the same room. Regarding this problem, one managing director also observed that, as a result of slimming down the organization, this problem had grown substantially worse as people became more and more stretched.

121

Shortage of meeting rooms

One other consequence of this slimming-down process was that companies had closed several offices and had cut down office overheads. The result was that, even once some dates had been found for meetings, frequently there were no meeting rooms free. Many simply delayed meetings until a room was available. Others who were more enterprising and results-driven started organizing project team meetings in the pub! Yet others started hijacking meeting rooms by turning up early and saying that they were already booked!

The unempowered representative

Having finally gathered their project teams together, many of the project leaders we interviewed thought their problems were over! They had visions of effective meetings where decisions would be made by those present and progress would follow. Many were shocked to find that the people attending these project meetings were reluctant to commit themselves to decisions without referring back to their departments. They hadn't thought that they, as project leaders, might have a role in negotiating people's authority levels with their respective line managers. They hadn't thought to ask the line managers involved to attend certain meetings which would make decisions which would affect them. Once again, delay and increasing frustration were the inevitable results.

Prevention is better than cure

What might be done to alleviate some of these problems? Some of the responsibility must lie with senior managers. Many have no idea of the amount of resources being committed to project working, no idea of the range of projects under way at any one time, or mechanisms for tracking which are on target or behind target. At a minimum, a senior manager initiating a project needs to encourage the chosen project leader to discuss where this project should rank in priority in relation to other projects that he/she is managing. Unless the management style and culture of the organization can accommodate this type of discussion, there is very little hope of stemming the huge haemorrhage of wasted resources. Another parallel activity is to provide project leaders with simple training in how to set priorities and how to manage their time effectively. Many of them were inexperienced in keeping several balls in the air simultaneously, and the stress of this tended to make them even less effective.

Another role for senior management is to act as mentors to young project leaders to help them to understand how the organization works, how decisions are made and where they are made, how to influence and persuade effectively, what they can do themselves, and where they need to negotiate support from someone more senior. Simple coaching of this kind can help project leaders to avoid wasting many frustrating weeks trying to discover the impenetrable rules of organizational life.

Senior management must also try to make at least some rough estimates of the resource requirements to be committed to organizational projects, otherwise they must accept that some projects will not go ahead. All projects suffer if teams cannot be assembled quickly enough. Slippage and inefficiencies easily become the norm, and this is very difficult to remedy.

However, part of the solution is for project leaders themselves to become a bit more street-wise. Get to know key decision-makers' secretaries, for example. They can give you very good insights into how to get things done and how to short-circuit decision-making processes. They usually also control the booking of meeting rooms, and a word in their ear can often secure space, particularly where meetings are booked well in advance. Schedule team meetings well ahead of time, not only to secure a room, but more importantly, to make sure that people are available. If you can ensure that meetings are entered in people's diaries, they usually become a priority. Our approaches to training project leaders are increasingly based around helping them learn such managerial and organizational skills.

Traditional project plans, particularly those developed by less-experienced project leaders, simply fail to reflect the time and resources required to resolve some of these issues. Allocating contingency is simply no substitute for being realistic about some of these less visible activities that lie behind the success of a project. They need to be made visible and estimated realistically, and creative ways need to be found to eliminate problems at source.

Keeping the task on track

The tools for control and monitoring and ways of motivating your team will depend on the nature of the project. What works for one type of project may not be suitable for another. For example, a well-defined project with clear, hard success criteria and a highly-visible full-time team mean that you are able to use far more clear-cut systems than will be appropriate to a more open project with only part-time team members.

The seduction of software

The arrival of sophisticated project-planning software has been a mixed blessing. In particular, it can become so fascinating and addictive that it eats up more time than it saves. Also, as more and more projects are less than concrete and are dynamic in nature, keeping data up-to-date as the project evolves rapidly can be a headache. Also, it is frequently simply too complicated and provides unnecessary

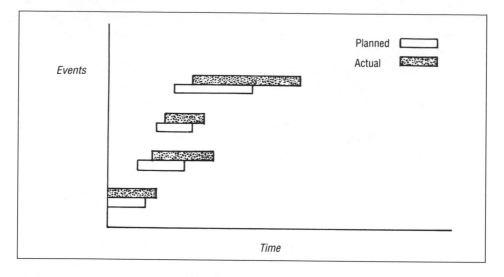

Planned

Actual

Events

Time

Figure 8.1 Gantt Chart

levels of sophistication.

As recently as ten years ago, project leaders would have seen the use of sophisticated software as the prerequisite for success in implementing a project. Today, however, a number of important riders would be added:

- such systems must *not* be seen to *control* the project, but to *provide information* to *enable* the project team to manage the project effectively
- such systems must be *simple* to operate and understand, and must *not* be an end in themselves
- such systems must be used with the *full support* of the project team, who must have confidence in the validity of the information being generated and in the way particular targets are set and monitored; they must *not* feel threatened by the system.

These must be the criteria in the new world of managing projects. There is a time and place for sophisticated software on complex, concrete projects with many tasks. There is also a time and place for using the software as a disciplined aid to thinking through how the different tasks and activities are related to each. Some of the simpler mouse-operated systems can certainly help in this regard. However, many project leaders use the simplest of monitoring and planning techniques, such as the Gantt Chart (see Figure 8.1). The technique is so simple, so flexible and so visual that it has many uses, including that of planning the 'What' for project team start-up (see Chapter 6, pp. 98–102). It summarizes the whole project on one sheet of paper – a vital function when explaining it to sponsors, stakeholders, team members and others. So, to summarize, keep it simple!

Plan–Do–Review cycles

Projects are dynamic and cannot be subject to rigid procedures. However, you do need to keep track of events and costs, so that you can make modifications as the project progresses. The function of project control systems is to provide the project team with reliable information on which to base decisions. The better the information, the better the decisions. Every project leader needs to decide which areas or activities are critical and need to be monitored closely if the project is to succeed, and which are not. For example, in a project to develop a new drug, it is obviously essential to set and monitor stringent quality control standards. You cannot disregard test results in order to achieve your budget. On the other hand, if you are responsible for an office move, it is unlikely that you will ever get everyone to agree on the colour of the tiles in the toilets – you have to take a decision based on a reasonable degree of consultation, and then press ahead.

With an open project, where the objective is less clear, and where strict control of resources is perhaps inappropriate, it is nevertheless important to set some overall targets. For example, if a group of people are meeting informally to see how they might be able to improve customer care in a certain area, then it is important to set some specific intermediate goals in order to maintain momentum; otherwise commitment levels will gradually fall away.

One drawback of the term 'project control system' is that it implies inflexibility. It creates the idea that, having made a plan, all you have to do is to control the project in accordance with it, and success will be inevitable. Of course, this is not so: very often the more high-performing a team is, the more it wishes to deviate from the original plan and improve the specification as it goes along. In practice, what happens is that a good project team and an effective leader, constantly modify the project's specification as it develops. They check the changes with the stakeholders, identify any problems, re-plan where necessary, and renegotiate resources and support if required. These activities can only be carried out if you are aware of the project's progress. Today's projects need something more than planning control systems. They need planning review systems to enable the project to move forward (see Figure 8.2).

These 'plan–do' review cycles are extremely important in maintaining the commitment of stakeholders and the interest of the team. Being in control of the process in a way which enables the project's performance specification to be improved will encourage stakeholders.

In effect, the implementation phase is a series of continuous Plan–Do–Review cycles, with the centre of gravity gradually moving forward, as shown in Figure 8.3.

As each activity is tested, and receives the support of the sponsor and the other stakeholders, the team develops a cohesiveness in the way it works, and becomes more confident in pressing forward with the project. It starts to face the uncertainties which arise in any project with a much greater degree of purpose.

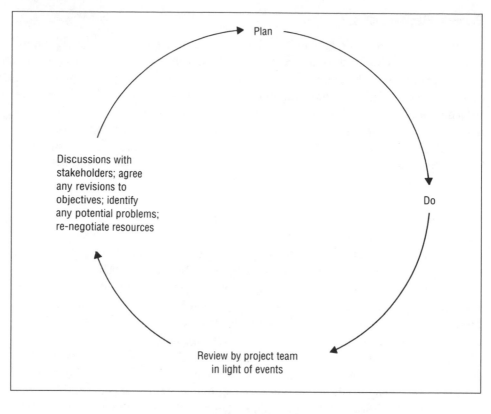

Figure 8.2 Planning/review system

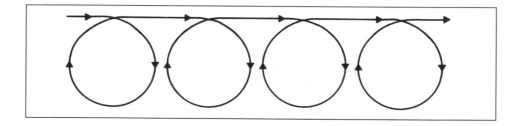

Figure 8.3 Plan–Do–Review cycles

A framework has developed for dealing with such matters.

Identification of intermediate targets (milestones)

Whilst the concept of continuous 'Plan–Do–Review' cycles provides a useful framework within which to work, you need to identify the points in the project which delineate each cycle. Not every element of a project is equally crucial to its success, and you need to identify at the outset which ones are. It is particularly important to identify those tasks which must be completed before another can begin. This identification process also provides motivation for individual team members. Once this has been done, you can set up the appropriate monitoring processes.

We discuss below four categories which affect success and need to be monitored.

Critical event-times or bottlenecks

Critical event times and bottlenecks occur in all aspects of the project. Some will be within your own direct control or be capable of being directly monitored by you. Others will occur in the work of subcontractors, or outside your direct knowledge. Different systems and procedures will be needed for different situations.

For example, the successful execution of a building project depends on component parts being ordered at the right time. A temporary project, such as the development of a strategic plan, may require you to meet the timetable of a series of meetings, each of which may deal with elements of strategy, if you are to arrive at the boardroom with a comprehensive plan.

Costs incurred and resources used

Like time, costs and resources are elements which need to be monitored continually. Normally, these are identified in the project plan. Sometimes cost limits are very clearly set out and relatively easy to monitor. On other occasions cost limits are not well specified, and extra costs may be permissible if certain results are achieved. This can all be spelt out in a project cost plan agreed at the outset. Projects at the open end of the continuum generally don't have any specific cost limits.

Direct costs are fairly easy to identify and monitor – usually using a monetary measure. Other types of resources are not so easy to identify and track. Take specialist skills or materials needed at certain points in the project: have these been identified at the outset? Have you decided how to check on their availability and their usage? Appropriate monitoring procedures need to be established for any items of this nature.

Quality assurance or performance specification

Concrete projects have quality assurance and performance specifications set in the original project definition. The success of open projects often depends as much on *how* you do things as on *what* you do. It is important to be very clear as to who is the most important party to satisfy on a particular quality target or performance specification: who has set the standard to be achieved? Is it the client or the end user, or even a third party such as a regulatory body? Alternatively, you and the project team may have set your own performance specifications. This will determine how you monitor a particular quality target and

127

the degree to which you could vary the specification if necessary. For example, there may be hard specifications set down by a regulatory body, from which you cannot deviate, while end users may be fairly flexible in some aspects of their final requirements.

Expectations of stakeholders

Individual stakeholders establish their own success criteria, well-defined in some types of project, less so in others. For example, the development of a corporate strategy plan is a very ill-defined project, with the individuals concerned possibly having differing personal objectives. You must know these in order to identify the elements which need to be monitored.

Keeping the team members on track

Deciding what items you need to monitor, and how you're going to monitor them, is only one aspect of keeping your project on track. The information provided by such monitoring systems has to be put to good use by the project team – there is no point in having first-class information if the team continues to operate inefficiently.

Ideally, a project team develops its own momentum and energy, and drives the project forward with commitment and enthusiasm; they trust their colleagues to back them up, and actively promote the Plan–Do–Review philosophy outlined earlier in this chapter. In concrete projects, when the team members are very visible and come together often, this level of teamworking is fairly easy to develop; people are accustomed to handling problems and conflicts which surface in meetings. But in temporary or open projects with less visible teams, identification of potential problems or conflict areas is much more difficult. People who disagree with the way the project is going, or who are encountering their own local difficulties, tend just to shelve the issue or give up and hope the problems will go away. It is at this end of the project spectrum that the project leader's personal leadership skills and style are really put to the test.

One way of thinking about how you can keep your team's motivation and performance high is to think of the team under two headings:

- *The team together* How can you get the best out of them when the team meets? What actions can you take to make the meetings more productive?
- *The team apart* How can you maintain momentum when they are not meeting regularly? Do you keep in touch with the team members, and support them when they need you?

The team together

There are always project meetings – regular in the case of concrete projects, occasional with less defined projects. Effective meetings don't just happen. They have to be worked at. Your first job is to ask the question: 'Is this meeting really necessary?'

Regular meetings are not ends in themselves. They can turn into tedious rituals if they have no real purpose. There are three main reasons to call a meeting: to communicate information, to solve problems and to make decisions.

From your point of view, meetings also serve a number of important underlying purposes:

- They create identity, cohesion and a sense of 'togetherness – meetings help to make the team visible.
- They help to make team members feel involved in discussing and arriving at decisions – which in turn produces a sense of ownership and commitment to those decisions.
- They develop synergy – the creative energy that helps the team achieve more collectively than individual members could on their own.
- They help to reinforce the team's ground rules. Meetings are times when these rules are seen in action and are reviewed, renewed or enforced.
- They provide an opportunity for teams to celebrate their successes together – generating and sustaining good morale, and revitalizing team members after intense periods of work.

Whatever the type of project, you will probably find it necessary to schedule some regular meetings of all team members. These help to keep the project on track.

It is crucial that you use these review meetings in two different ways. The first is the traditional feedback route – looking at what has actually happened, comparing it with the plan, and working on resultant problems. But probably a more powerful technique, and certainly one that is used infrequently in our experience, is to *preview* – to anticipate what is coming up, to *feed forward* problems and blockages that team members foresee. In this way you can solve problems before they occur, or at least have the opportunity to minimize their consequences and carry out damage limitation exercises in advance. Remember, everyone involved with projects tends to hate nasty surprises that come out of the blue. Forewarned is forearmed. However, day-to-day issues may have to be resolved by other meetings, often impromptu or at short notice. These may not involve all the team, but just those who need to talk about something together.

Meetings may also not always involve – or be led by – you! Effective delegation is part of good team leadership.

Meetings – The ten 'golden rules'

To help you in your task, we have prepared what we regard as the ten essential

129

rules for running meetings successfully:

- *Preparation* Circulate an agenda and relevant papers sufficiently in advance to allow team members to read and prepare. Take into account any preparation or recommendations of sub-groups created in past meetings.
- *Purpose* Think carefully, if appropriate with other team members, about what you want out of the meeting. Make sure everyone is quite clear why they are there.
- *Time scheduling* Structure the available time to ensure an appropriate airing for each issue. Encourage brevity to help achieve everything on the agenda.
- *Create understanding* Try to ensure good communication between team members by *listening* actively to others and responding to what they say; by *asking for clarification* to clear up confusion, and by *summarizing* to keep the group on the right track and check for understanding. Encourage other team members to do the same. You only learn when you listen, not when you talk.
- *Staying on track* Stick to the agenda and stop team members (or yourself!) from wandering off the subject. Do not allow team members to introduce personal hobby horses or red herrings.
- *Use diverse experience and skills* Encourage the active participation of *all* team members, especially the quieter ones. Avoid dominating the discussion yourself or giving too much time to contributions from over-assertive team members.
- *Creative problem-solving* Encourage the team not to take 'no' for an answer. Discourage expressions such as 'can't', 'musn't' and 'impossible' in favour of 'what if', 'how' and 'there must be a way to'. Use the full diversity of the team as a source of ideas.
- *Check for agreement* Don't assume that silence means consent. Check everyone for agreement, particularly on important decisions to which widespread commitment is important.
- *Review the working of the team* Encourage brief but honest feedback about performance at the end of each meeting. Ensure that basic ground rules are still appropriate and working well.
- *Action* Ensure that all actions agreed at the meeting are summarized and understood. Identify clearly the individuals responsible and ensure that realistic deadlines are specified. Circulate this summary in writing to all concerned within twenty-four hours to act as a reminder.

One last idea is to build in enough 'silly time'. When members of a team have been apart for a long time they often need to get to know each other again and re-form the team. You should allow some informal time for this 'bonding' process to take place. We call it 'silly time' because it is often spent catching up on gossip and exchanging lighthearted banter. But it is important.

Remember that meetings represent valuable time, and are held to help keep the project on track and moving towards completion.

The team apart: Some more 'golden rules'

As we said earlier, the real work of teams takes place outside meetings. In some types of project the number of formal meetings is actually very small, although there may be a number of *ad hoc* meetings. There is no point in agreeing a series of actions at meetings if all that occurs at the next meeting is a series of carefully thought-out explanations of why individual team members have failed to carry them out. A large part of the responsibility for ensuring that they are carried out falls on your shoulders.

Here is a second set of rules to follow:

- *Who does what and when* Before the team leaves the meeting, make sure that everyone has a clear idea of what they have been mandated to do, in terms of actions and results within a specified period of time. Encourage each member to see themselves as a team ambassador, entrusted with the responsibility of managing those outside the team with whom they come into contact.

- *Holding on and letting go* Encourage each team member to hold on to the lines of support you have created but at the same time to let go of your apron strings and work responsibly alone. At the same time, make sure that you let go of team members. Trust individuals to meet deadlines, trust their commitment, and let go of the tasks you have delegated to them. Interference through distrust or anxiety will produce a negative reaction.

- *Protect members from distractions* Even with full-time team members, events sometimes occur outside the team's work which require a response from an individual team member. If possible, try to act as a shield for them by handling some of the pressure. Encourage them to approach you if they need support. At the other extreme, where the project is a part-time activity, team members need encouragement from you to avoid your project being seen as just a distraction.

- *Maintain momentum and commitment* It is far easier to create excitement at the start of a project than to keep generating it when the team is working apart. You can help to sustain momentum by providing team members with constant reminders of their priorities. This is particularly true of part-time members who have conflicting responsibilities. Without interfering with the work of team members, you must try to keep them motivated. Keep in touch with each member, be available when needed, and provide support. If the pressure is too great, you may need to renegotiate success criteria with the sponsor or client or make some kind of deal with those who control other aspects of the team member's responsibilities. Even if the team is unhindered by outside commitments, you still need to maintain momentum by finding ways to show each of the members how valuable their contribution is and by reminding them of how their part fits into the Big Picture. Open projects, with less structured reporting, require you to make special efforts to maintain momentum.

- *Create active communications* Your role when the team is apart is rather like a spider weaving a web. You are at the centre, but you are constantly making the links between one point and another by staying in touch with individuals and passing information between different members and between them and the centre. Tom Peters, co-author of *In Search of Excellence*, termed this 'management by walking about' (MBWA).
- *Create 'early warning' systems* A major cause of project failure is where problems are not foreseen, or worse, where a problem is foreseen by one team member but hidden from the others because of worry over apportionment of blame. Encourage the adoption of a ground rule that *any* problem encountered by any team member, particularly if it might affect others, is to be signalled to you early. Create a blame-free atmosphere where it is acceptable to share problems, to ask for help and to admit to being stuck. Encourage the frequent, fast and frank exchange of information and the idea that it is a cardinal sin to let another team member down.

Keeping the stakeholders in the picture

We have stressed the need to ensure that project monitoring systems are appropriate to the task and generate the appropriate information to enable the team to perform at the highest level, whether together or apart. This keeps your project on track and enables you to keep stakeholders informed of progress, so that they remain committed to the project and feel part of the team. Even if the sponsor, client and end user are unable to attend your project meetings frequently, they must be kept fully informed and able to communicate with team members.

In a concrete project, the main stakeholders often attend all project meetings and have instant access to all necessary information. In other types of project, you may have to make special efforts to keep in touch, employing the most appropriate methods. Do they like informal chats over a cup of coffee or pint of beer? Or do they need regular presentations with slides or graphs? What is the best method of getting them involved in the project? Perhaps a site visit, or involvement in a prototype demonstration?

All contacts with stakeholders enable you to pick up signals, both explicit and implicit, on how they see the project developing and whether their expectations are changing. For example, if end users are excited by seeing the possibilities of a new computerized information system, encourage them to talk to their boss (the client) about any enhancements they would like to see. Get them on your side, make them part of your team and committed to your project.

Conclusion

Keeping a project on track involves not just agreeing a plan, issuing instructions and checking to see that everything is being carried out accordingly. It's a matter of the project leader being acutely aware of the subtle but significant shifts of opinion, desires or expectations of the people who make up the project team and stakeholders. You have to keep the monitoring systems finely tuned, and you have to encourage consensus and team development in relation to an ever changing objective. The process of implementation is challenging and exhilarating. There's a tremendous sense of achievement when you come to hand over the project.

9 Handing over and winding up

Even when a project appears to be completed, there is often much work still to do. Quality experts tell us that the cost of re-work due to mistakes, oversights and poor processes is often about 25% of the original production costs. There are sad stories of computer departments spending around 80% of their total investment in software development on patching and maintaining creaking systems. So the after-life of a project is important.

Three aspects of the project's after-life show how successful its leader has been:

- Ensure that the client organization is linked into the project so that they can use it confidently. Few leaders start this process soon enough or put enough effort into it.
- Audit the project life cycle and processes, building on strengths and attacking the weaknesses identified. Individual and organizational learning results from an audit. Experience without review means that mistakes are liable to be repeated.
- Dismantle the organizational team and move on, celebrating and enjoying the success of the project, so that you and your team feel rewarded and recognized for your achievements.

Letting go is not as easy as it sounds. You may well have built up a sense of ownership of the project over the months or years it has taken to bring it to completion. You may be reluctant to see it taken over until you are sure it is really fulfilling its purpose. This can often cause difficulties with the client, who is, after all, the real owner and beneficiary.

Maintaining high performance to the last minute can be a problem. Keeping the momentum going is tough. Team members who were very effective at finding new ways of doing things in the beginning may not be nearly so interested in the detailed documentation necessary to hand over a workable system.

The following guidelines for this final stage aim to help you become a project leader with a high reputation for seeing the job through to lasting performance.

The problem of handing over

If you've followed our approach of involving all main stakeholders early in the project life cycle, then you will have started the handover process at the beginning of the project and the final handover should contain no surprises. The difficulty is in the new relationship with the client. The client is no longer specifying results and setting policy guidelines; the client at this stage becomes the actual user, operator or consumer of your project's product or service. The client has to live with the results, day in day out. The client needs to know the detail of how it's going to work.

The 'client' is, in fact, likely to appear in the form of numerous users. So, suddenly your project team has to relate to an army of other teams. The logistics of this absorb a considerable amount of time and are very important. Users are a long way behind you in their familiarity with the project. Yet now they have to live with it.

Remember where you came from ...

It helps if you try to understand the newcomers who have to be linked into the project to give it a strong healthy life:

- Remember that it's all clear to you because you've lived with it for weeks, months or years.
- Remember what it was like when you were groping in the early stages to get to grips with the complexity of it all.
- Remember that is where *they* are *now*.

It requires humility and patience to carry out the handover effectively at a time when team motivation may be slipping a little. You may already be looking beyond the current project to the next one.

Once the real users start to become active they find bugs, holes, gaps or unforeseen problems. This is true whether your project is building a house or a software package, whether it is a concrete project or an open one. There are always genuine, interesting questions to be solved at the end, because it is impossible to think of everything on the way. The question is how to reduce the shocks in number and severity.

The handover process for open projects can sometimes be difficult to manage because, by their very nature, the outcome is often uncertain. Sometimes there is nothing to show for the project except the knowledge that further work would be viable. On the other hand, an open project which is successful usually becomes either a temporary project, subject to a further tentative stage of development, or a concrete project. Many ideas for new product development start as 'skunk works', as some innovative firms call them, and go on to become concrete projects. To achieve this the project leader has to manage the sponsors and the political environment very actively to gain official status for the project.

Making handing over easier

Handover success is achieved by involving the users earlier than you might have supposed.

We stress this because handover is the point in the project life cycle where the uncertain areas between the project team and the client are greatest. Starting early and working for a long time to reduce the uncertainty means that fewer critical issues are left out. Even more important, it builds the sense of ownership and confidence of the client.

Some methods which can be used at the handover stage are set out below.

Build in link people

Give one team member the specific job of managing the handover. The client company should also have an implementation manager. Ensuring that 'heavyweight' people are charged with implementation prevents the handover being left to everybody and nobody. It signals that it is being taken seriously. It injects direct resources and commitment into this critical phase. It also ensures that detailed planning and control extend to the end of the project.

Bring support people into the team. These may be concerned with training, helpline services, maintenance, operating procedures, production of reference materials or troubleshooting. Start to integrate these people as soon as you have an outline or prototype which can give them an idea of what the end product might be like. They can start understanding and tuning in to the project before they have to respond rapidly to last-minute demands. It also builds their skill and competence without the risk involved in working with the final product. To gain a depth of understanding, they need to be part of the team, and not seen as additional extras or second-class members.

If you do not start this learning process early enough and don't invest enough time in preparing people – explaining, training, explaining again – then you may have to inject large quantities of resources to rescue the situation.

Concrete projects need a great deal of publicity and explaining at this stage, but temporary projects may need even more! For instance, if you are trying to help a company adopt a new strategic direction, you need to use all the marketing means possible to let people know *what* is changing and *why*. But this is only the first step. Understanding does not necessarily lead to action.

More support services

A few days' training, a newly-qualified trainer, a huge pile of technical operating manuals as a back-up – have you seen these being relied upon heavily as vehicles for handing over? It is a common pattern in many concrete projects where new machinery or systems are involved. If there are many users to train, this is time-consuming and complex. But it is nowhere near enough. Many new computer installations are underused or misused because the users are chronically undersupported. This produces a poor return on investment for the client, much frustration for the users, and tiresome emotional worries for the project leader.

Here are some ideas for enhancing the handover:

- Build up the introduction of the project to the users. Use presentation exhibitions, lunchtime meetings, demonstrations, models or tours.
- Provide several short training sessions – not one long one. Conduct small-group simulations of the work environment with all its pressures. Or, for temporary projects, discuss with the people involved the implications of the recommendations of the project team for their work. For example, in a customer service project, what does being more customer-orientated mean for the telephonist?
- Provide helpline support, so that somebody is readily available to sort out immediate problems. This is particularly important for people depending on new technology for the execution of their work.
- Use one-to-one or small-group training at the workplace. Talk through problems. Find out what can and cannot be done, and why. Many quality projects have found it is important to go through actual problems with the relevant core team.
- Build up a resource of specialist back-up that can be called in to deal with more technical questions or unexpected results. This is vital in concrete projects with high risks depending on equipment functioning reliably.
- Support and develop 'leading' users who work with other users but who are more experienced and can build the confidence of new users. They can talk the users' language and see the problems from their perspective. Quality experts or customer service focal points have been created as a result of temporary projects.
- Create a learning centre where individuals can work through particular questions or routines with guidance. Hold informal question/answer sessions to provide a safety valve for complaints or hidden problems.
- Write clear documentation, guides and handbooks which are user-friendly. Answer the questions naive users always wanted – but never dared – to ask. This is just as important for less concrete projects with ideas which are difficult to communicate.

If you constantly think about being user-friendly, the handover will be smoother because you will quickly see the problems, and avoid minor hitches. Listen to the mood of users, ask them what help they need, and react quickly and appropriately.

A process for handing over to users

A well-known computer systems company has developed a series of steps to be taken by their project teams when handing over systems to client support teams. This could be used for a wide range of concrete projects, and some temporary ones involving many people.

1. *Make them aware*: with written materials, presentations and informal discussions at least two months before introduction – in order to establish expectations of what is on the way.
2. *Get them interested*: with written materials, presentations and informal discussions at least one month prior to introduction – in order to clarify expectations and answer queries (what, when and why?). Show a mock-up, give a demonstration to give the client an idea of what will be involved.
3. *Reassure (What will happen to us?)*: through discussions with client co-ordinators, supervisors and end–users using documentation of prototypes. This should take place one or two weeks prior to introduction, and answer questions such as: 'How will the work change?', 'What will be expected of the work group, and what have others experienced?', 'What support will be provided?'
4. *Introduction*: the system is put into operation or a prototype exists.
5. *Formal training*: involving classroom training, demonstrations, individual practice and comparisons with existing systems (if any). Some of the most important items covered by the training should include:
   - gaining skills in using equipment
   - gaining knowledge of what is happening and how to handle links between activities
   - practising routines, and highlighting how to use manuals and self-help facilities
   - stress key points for accuracy and control
   - build troubleshooting processes to cope when things go wrong (what is really serious and must be avoided?)
6. *Practice, coaching and problem-solving*: designed to provide quick help in early stages of use, to help users to solve their own problems. These can be achieved through informal contacts, but should be friendly and readily available.
7. *Additional training*: undertaken in a classroom to correct frequent faults in use, make modifications and develop effective use of the system. Build up best practice. Sort out problems or identify the modifications needed.
8. *Review*: involving discussions with users and supervisors in order to assess the system's strengths and weaknesses and provide additional communication and training.

Auditing the project life cycle

Why worry when the project is dead? Why not let it rest in peace? Many project leaders feel that this is sensible. Picking over the past can be a morbid and recriminatory experience. But it does not need to be. You and your organization can learn a lot about what to do better next time. New best practices can be discovered, and they need to be communicated to all team leaders, members and sponsors. Persistent organizational or procedural problems can be dealt with, in order to secure improvements in performance. One project-based company asked itself why its projects were failing or producing disappointing performance. After auditing several projects, it found the common features or patterns of interaction which showed clearly what was cause and what was symptom. The company's failures were connected with:

- too many people working on too many projects
- frequent priority changes
- projects technically focused, with insufficient market sensitivity.

Many project-based companies working in software development find it difficult to estimate the time it will take to develop and test a defined piece of software. They underestimate. So they need to build up data about how long a project actually takes, using that as a standard for estimating and identifying where the blockages or deviations occur. As the experience of projects builds up, guesses and hypotheses are turned into reliable data.

Project audits usually reveal weaknesses in three areas – poor project definition, weak project sponsorship or bad project organization. A good project leader has nothing to fear from an audit.

Topics for a project audit

- Definition of success criteria
  - were they adequate?
  - how were they arrived at?
- Steps in the project life cycle
  - where was the team effective?
  - where were the problems?
- Project organization and control tools
  - did they help or hinder?
- What problems were encountered and how were they dealt with?
- Identify the information from as many directions as possible. Differentiate between symptoms and causes.
- Constraints that were surprising
- Links with stakeholders
  - strengths and weaknesses

140

● Organization and communication of the core team and project leader.

If you run an audit, it must be a participative problem-solving process with as many members of the organizational team as possible. (It should include the sponsor.) You need to hear all the views, so give your team members time to reflect on their experience in the project, and tell them prior to the meeting the sort of questions you have in mind. They can be encouraged to carry out mini-audits with their parts of the visible or invisible team. Your client should be included in some aspects of the audit. Input from the client will enable you to test some of your suggestions for improvement.

One of the dangers of audits is that people – project leaders especially – perceive them as witch hunts. But this fear can be overcome by making clear the audit's ground rules: concentrate on the issues and problems, not the personalities, and do not criticize or disapprove of anything unless you can offer something better in its place. We can all push things over. Rebuilding takes effort and genuine interest. Tap into ideas that the organizational team members have; they have first-hand experience of the problems, and may well have worked out the best solutions.

Once you have completed the audit, don't forget to let other project leaders or sponsors know what your experience has taught you. Your proposals on how to improve performance are valuable competitive information. Sharing best practice, informally and formally, is one of the most effective ways of spreading learning through the organization to improve its capacity for achieving results through projects. For instance, you can:

● send a summary of bad/good points with recommendations to senior management and other project leaders
● hold a briefing workshop to test ideas for improvement
● ensure that a comprehensive financial report is included, with real expenditure compared with original and revised estimates
● make sure others know why you have been successful – what you did differently. Success is rarely just the result of good luck.

Finally, ensure that you too learn from the review process. Each project you undertake or lead provides a significant learning experience which may well prove invaluable in your future career. Consider what you have learnt from your own experience. Try to be specific about the positive and negative events and how you handled them.

An example of a constructive project audit

The New Ventures Division of an international telecommunications organization was experiencing difficulty in bringing an important new product to the market fast enough and at a competitive price.

141

In discussing the issue, the management team realized that there had been several smaller projects over the previous five years which had not been successful either, apparently because of technical difficulties that were insuperable. One team member suggested that this was not really the reason for failure, but was just a face-saving formula that those involved knew would be acceptable to senior management.

The team, horrified by this suggestion, asked one of the previous project leaders to form a small group to analyse the past failures, so that the whole division could learn from them. The group worked rapidly and their report was circulated throughout the division within ten days.

The Divisional Director asked each member of the division to put forward ideas about how the lessons from the report could be applied constructively to their own project. Each project team then discussed these extensively and came up with its own 'performance improvement plan'. Each plan had two sections:

- things we can do ourselves
- things that the Divisional Service Management Team needs to do.

The latter issues were brought together by the Divisional Director and discussed by the senior team; plans for their resolution, with clear responsibilities and deadlines, were circulated to all.

Over the next six months some large changes were made, as well as a whole range of small ones by many people. Morale and confidence rose rapidly and progress towards meeting the main project objectives was generally recognized to have been substantially accelerated.

In our experience, it is surprisingly rare for an audit to be an integral part of the life cycle of a concrete project. We hope we have convinced you that it is worthwhile investing time and energy at the end of one project on an audit which will enhance the effectiveness of the next project.

Project audits are even less common in temporary projects. While it may be true that the project itself may not be repeated, the use of project teams to progress organizational problems should be continued, as they are a valuable way of developing a business. A forthright Personnel Director declared: 'Project teams don't help to solve the different interests of the corporate centre and the business units. Take the team that looked at equal opportunities.' It could not be disputed that the performance of the team had satisfied nobody. The report was vague and hurried. Meetings had been hard to get off the ground. Some people had never turned up. The business units refused to endorse the recommendations on the grounds that they were academic and impractical.

In our view, this Personnel Director was shooting at the wrong target. If he had asked how the team had been set up, what it had been expected to do, what priority it had been given, how much and what type of contribution it had needed from corporate experts and the business units, it would have been clear that the process of constituting the team had doomed it to failure. Unfortunately, no audit was carried out, so the organization concerned will never know! Temporary and open projects can use a project audit to increase their own and the organization's understanding of how teams can deal effectively with organizational questions.

Dismantling the project team

As the project approaches its conclusion, a good team will gain momentum. However, individual members often look further ahead and become concerned about their career development and position within the organization once the team is dismantled. Because of this, the elation of achievement can be speedily followed by depression. You need to help people understand this process, which is illustrated by the 'moodograph' in Figure 9.1.

A celebration held at the end of a project helps people to get the most out of its success. It is a chance to recognize the work, not only of the team's leaders, but of all its members, both visible and invisible. The end of a project is an emotional event, and a celebration – however small – of its success helps people to come to terms with the change occurring in their life.

The future for team members may well depend on their personal performance and the credibility of the project. If you have been successful, other project leaders may be trying to snap up your people before you are really ready to let them go. You will have some tough decisions to make. Letting somebody who is important to you take up a new post at this stage could be your last visible sign of commitment and support to that team member. It is important to start openly discussing with members what they would prefer to do, what their strengths are, how they might develop or improve, and what you think the realistic alternatives are for them in the organization. One-to-one counselling sessions can provide reassurance and moral support.

To prevent unnecessary apprehension, you should make sure that the sponsor and any other relevant senior executive has planned the future role of project team members well before the end of the project. This must be done and the conclusions communicated to team members in sufficient time to avoid loss of motivation. You need to have established who in the organization is responsible for making decisions on the future use of staff; contact them, promote the achievements of your team members and keep the pressure on to make sure that they are properly rewarded. If you leave redeployment to the last minute, the organization may make hasty decisions that are disadvantageous to itself and to the individuals concerned.

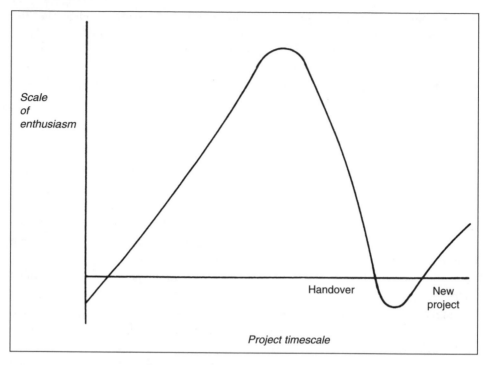

Scale of enthusiasm

Handover

New project

Project timescale

Figure 9.1   **The project 'moodograph'**

What about you?

What have you learnt from this project that tells you where you want to go next, or the sort of project you are seeking next? If people who matter don't talk to you, perhaps you should let them know, using the audit report, what you have contributed.

Some months before your project comes to an end you may need to start reminding sponsors and decision-makers that you will be available. Organizations which work with a project management structure are usually well aware of beginnings and ends of projects. So the issue in this case will be to put together your negotiating position on the basis of what you would prefer to do and the type of challenge you are ready to take on. If you are seen to have been successful, you can often afford to be forceful in ensuring that your next project will be set up with conditions that you know will help it to succeed. If you are not a shining star in the organization, review your own strengths and see where you need to build your expertise and organizational visibility. Think through the three dimensions set out in Chapter 1 (p. 18) in terms of what has happened in your project. How would you tackle things differently?

Temporary projects are very different in that you are likely to have retained your normal job throughout, and have worked only part-time on the project. Therefore, you have no expectation of a totally new job. Temporary projects often give both leaders and members a wider view of the organization and its operating environment, as well as access to a wider network of important political influences. So, when a project ends, it is sometimes rather unexciting to resume business as usual. Reflecting on your own and/or talking to senior managers or mentors about what you have learnt can help you to capitalize on your experience. Understanding how certain ideas can be applied constructively to other situations is one way of moving from a functional to a more general management outlook. You may have discovered other aspects of your organization that you would be interested to explore further. Let your manager know of your preferences at performance appraisal time or through informal discussions.

If you do not move on to new pastures, applying the broader perspective of organizational networking and the integrative processes of project leadership will help you to improve your 'home team'.

Conclusion

This chapter has highlighted a number of aspects of the handover and winding up processes:

- the withdrawal of the project team and the phasing-in of the long-term stable team
- keeping the momentum of the project team going until the end, even when interest and enthusiasm are threatening to decline
- the project audit, to build on experience
- the future of team members and – most important – of their leader.

Part IV
Action Summary

In this section we pull the whole book together in summary form with a page per chapter of key points, key questions and, where appropriate, additional reading for further investigation of the topic.

Introduction: The brave new world of project management

Key points

- New-style projects operate in areas beyond the traditional criteria of time, cost and specification, and are concerned with a variety of tasks within the context of an organization.
- They involve a wide range of stakeholders, organizational 'politics', the external environment, marketing pressures and the complex needs and objectives of a large number of individuals.
- The new-style leader therefore needs a broader perspective.
- New-style projects are an important mechanism for creating co-operation across boundaries, both within the organization and across different organizations.

Key questions

- What are the different ways in which your organization is using project teams?
- How many people in your organization could be said to be project leaders (they almost certainly won't have a title like that) or project team members?
- In general, how successful are these projects thought to be, and what differentiates the good from the bad?

Additional reading

- Hastings, C., 1993, *The New Organization: Growing the Culture of Organizational Networking*, McGraw-Hill, Maidenhead.
- Hastings, C., et al., 1986, *Superteams: Building Organisational Success Through High Performing Teams*, HarperCollins, London.
- Lipnack, J. & Stamps, J., 1994, *The Teamnet Factor: Bringing the Power of Boundary Crossing into your Organization*, Oliver Wright Publications, Essex Junction, VT 05452, USA.

Chapter 1: What makes a good project leader?

Key points

- The project leader's role is exposed and visible. It frequently involves working in areas which are new for the organization, which causes conflicts. The role is complex – some say impossible!
- The three demands of the role are to manage the stakeholders (through looking upwards and outwards), to manage the project life cycle (through looking forwards and backwards) and to manage performance (through looking inwards and downwards).
- Being an integrator means using specific processes to help you keep things together and going in the right direction. The fourteen integrative processes highlight what you need to focus on and give you ideas as to how you might do it.

Key questions

- Have you completed the questionnaire at the end of Chapter 1? What are your strengths and blind spots? Talk to colleagues and team members – what do they say?
- Which of the integrative processes might help you to identify alternative strategies?
- Are you taking care of yourself? What do you enjoy in the project leadership role? What winds you up? What are your early warning signals that might help you to feel as if you are staying on top of things?
- Think of how you spend your time. Do you attend to difficult technical questions to the exclusion of wider issues? How much time do you spend with your team? How often do you talk to key stakeholders.

Additional reading

- Gareis, R., 1990, *Managing by Project* Mainz, Vienna.

Chapter 2: The project in the organization

Key points

- There are different types of project, depending on:
  - the extent to which the output can be defined at the beginning
  - the level of structure and formality need
  - the level of know-how that exists in the organization.
- Projects can be classified as concrete, occasional or open, and the approach to project management needs to be designed to be appropriate to the project type.
- You may find that, as a project leader, you prefer one type of project to another, since it suits your natural capabilities best.

Key questions

- How would you classify the projects you are working on? Have you developed the most suitable management approach to deal with the particular issues of this project? Or are you adopting standard procedures that do not seem to work well?
- How would you discuss the type of projects you are working on with your immediate boss and team members? Do you recognize some of the characteristics in Figures 2.2, 2.3 and 2.4?
- Looking back on projects you have been involved with, which type of projects do you prefer to lead? Which aspects of each project make you feel confident, and where are there areas for potential development?

Additional reading

- Moss Kanter, R., 1983, *The Change Masters: Corporate Entrepreneurs at Work*, Unwin, London.
- Senge, P., 1992, *The Fifth Discipline*, Century Business, London.

Chapter 3: Understanding the Big Picture

Key points

- No project is an island, there is always a desired impact that the project deliverables should achieve. Can you explain what the difference is between the deliverables and the impact of your project?
- Understanding the organizational Big Picture enables the project leader to communicate why this project is important. The dimension of visibility indicates how prominent organizational politics are likely to be in the project.
- High-visibility projects tend to mean that a project leader must actively engage with political management to ensure the organizational environment will support project success.
- Different projects pose different risks, in terms of the number of uncertain elements and their scope of potential damage, plus the probability of occurrence. Project leaders need to map these together with their sponsor in the early stages of undertaking a project. Once you have anticipated the 'hot spots' you can plan actions to limit damages, rather than being unpleasantly surprised.

Key questions

- What are the main factors that influence your project's deliverables – competitive moves, customer pressures, environmental changes or internal performance questions? Can you explain the make-up of your project team convincingly, and how your project contributes to one or more of these aspects?
- How visible is your project? What sort of political dynamics can you anticipate? What help do you need to manage these actively?
- With your sponsor, map the project risks, use the checklist in Figure 3.6 to help you. Make the worst possible situations explicit. If you can contain these, then you will easily master lesser disruptions! Plan how to handle the major risks and decide what the most appropriate project structure, estimating and planning tools are. In particular, decide how to build the stakeholder support needed in the prevailing political climate. Different project types need to be managed by attending to the technical questions and the organizational resistance that will occur.

Additional reading

- Hamal, G. & Prahalad, C. K., 1994, *Competing for the Future*, Harvard Business Publications, Boston.
- Quinn Mills, D., 1991, *Rebirth of the Corporation*, John Wiley, New York.

Chapter 4: Managing the sponsor

Key points

- The sponsor and project leader need to build a collaborative working relationship to ensure that the project is successful. This need increases if the project is more open or visible. You have to work together to manage the stakeholders.
- This relationship is new for both parties and cuts across a normal hierarchical line management relationship. So you need to discuss explicitly the type of sponsorship that the project needs. Manage upwards constantly.
- Projects cause organizational change, which in turn stimulates 'political' activity. This is natural and inevitable, but the project leader has to learn how to read the political patterns of the organization and manage his/her own style and its appropriateness.

Key questions

- How good is your relationship with your sponsor? Are you jointly running the project effectively? Review aspects of the relationship. How do you help and hinder each other? Discuss this at the next project review. Have you understood your expectations of each other?
- What are the 'political' patterns or games in the organizational context around your project? What typically happens? What has undermined previous projects? Can you learn from these?
- Are you an Owl, Monkey, Elephant or Sheep? Where does this help? What do you do when you feel wrong-footed? What alternatives might there be?

Additional reading

- James, K. & Baddeley, S., 1987, 'Owl, Fox, Donkey or Sheep: Political Skills for Managers', *Management Education & Development*, Vol. 18.
- Lynch, D. & Kordis, P., 1990, *Strategy of the Dolphin*, Arrow Books, London.
- Stacey, R., 1992, *Managing Chaos*, Kogan Page, London.
- Stewart, I. & Joines, V., 1987, *Today,* Lifespan Publishing, Nottingham.

Chapter 5: Scoping

Key points

- Scoping has overt and covert purposes, which include defining what is included and what is not included in the project, as well as building the stakeholders' confidence in the project leader. Poor scoping is the source of most project problems.
- Five critical questions should be answered in the scoping process:
  - What is the business rationale for the project?
  - What do different stakeholders expect of the project?
  - What will it involve us in doing?
  - Do we have what's necessary to do it?
  - What do we want to happen as a result of the project?

  Answering these helps you make the case for the project.
- There are a number of simple tools for scoping.

Key questions

- Are you always under early pressure to 'get on with the project'? This should alert you to possible scoping problems.
- Can you answer the five scoping questions for the project you are involved in? If not, why not?
- Decide which scoping tools may be useful for you, and try them out on your project.

Additional reading

- Fisher, R. & Ury, W., 1983, *Getting to Yes: Negotiating Agreement Without Giving In*, Hutchinson, London.

Chapter 6: The project start-up

Key points

- Effective team working does not always happen naturally. Part of your role as project leader is to take steps to ensure that your team starts to work effectively as rapidly as possible.
- Part of this concerns ensuring the right mix of people to fit the project type (although this is not always in your control).
- Explicit team start-up activities accelerate team formation. These broadly involve working together on planning what the team is trying to achieve, and how it will need to operate.

Key questions

- How clear are all your team members about why the organization wants your project and precisely what impact it is designed to achieve? Do they *really* understand it?
- What specific actions have you taken to influence how effectively your team members work together, or have you just hoped for the right chemistry?
- Have you discussed any of the issues in Exercises 1–3 at the end of Chapter 6 with your team members? Answers to these questions unlock many of the keys to individual motivation.

Additional reading

- Hastings, C., Bixby, P. and Chaudhry-Lawton, R., 1986, *Superteams: Building Organisational Success Through High Performing Teams*, HarperCollins, London.
- Katzenbach, J. & Smith, D., 1993, *The Wisdom of Teams*, Harvard Business School Press, Boston.

Chapter 7: 'Marketing' to the stakeholders

Key points

- Marketing concepts help us to make visible the tasks that need to be undertaken to run a project with the stakeholders in mind. Once the market segments or stakeholder groups are identified, then they can be made aware of the project benefits in terms they find attractive.
- The project leader needs to have an internal marketing plan to build effective working relationships with key stakeholders. These run throughout the project, and need people, time and money to resource them. Otherwise, 'communication' is seen as a side issue and not an integral part of the project.
- Informal marketing or networking is as important as formal activities. However, it cannot be left to chance, so networking activities need to be agreed with team members, as they represent the project whenever they talk to stakeholders.

Key questions

- How can you cluster your stakeholders into market segments? What are the benefits they hope to gain from the project? How will you deliver to them or engage them? What has been their experience of the 'moments of truth' so far?
- What project culture do you currently have? How would you describe it? And, more important, how would market segments of stakeholding view it? To what extent are the ground rules explicit and adhered to? How do they support the project's image?
- What does your internal marketing plan look like? Have you planned enough informal contact with key stakeholders? What is the mix between formal and informal activities? Does the medium fit the message you want to put across?
- Who is good at networking in your team? How can you extend the alternative ways of networking to build confidence and credibility in the project?

Additional reading

- Christopher, M., Payne, A. & Ballantyne, D., 1992, *Relationship Marketing,* Butterworth-Heinemann, Oxford.
- Hastings, C., 1993, *The New Organization: Growing the Culture of Organizational Networking,* McGraw-Hill, Maidenhead.
- Moss Kanter, R., 1983, *The Change Masters: Corporate Entrepreneurs at Work,* Unwin, London.

Chapter 8: Keeping on track

Key points

- The real world has a habit of getting in the way of the best-laid plans. The art of leading a project is to get back on track quickly.
- There are many insidious ways in which slippage can occur. Being aware of these can help you to control them.
- There are many complex and simple tools to help you keep on track. Choose appropriate ones; in general, the simpler the better.
- Don't try to keep track of everything yourself. Use all team members by bringing them together in planned review meetings with the accent on looking *forwards*, to anticipate problems before they occur.

Key questions

- How do your projects come to be derailed? Analyse the causes so that you can pre-empt them next time.
- How clear are you about what basic information you and the team need to keep control of progress? Don't overcomplicate it.
- Are your project review meetings constructive and problem-solving or blaming and scapegoating sessions? How can you make them motivating rather than de-motivating for team members?

Additional reading

- Andersen, E., Grude, K. Haug, T. and Rutner, R., 1987, *Goal Directed Project Management*, Kogan Page, London.
- Peters, T. and Waterman, R., 1982, *In Search of Excellence*, Harper & Row, New York.
- The Open College, 1993, *Managing Projects: A Distance Learning Package*, Manchester, Tel: +44 161 434 0007.

Chapter 9: Handing over and winding up

Key points

- Develop a structured programme to involve end users and any operational support staff as early as possible in the handover. In particular, build in a process to publicize the Big Picture so that users understand why the project is necessary.
- Project audits are an invaluable management tool, helping you to identify the good and the not-so-good elements of a project, which will make the next project that much better.
- At this stage in the project life cycle, the project leader must look after the interests of the team members when the project finishes.

Key questions

- How did you communicate your project to the end users and operational support team? Was it reasonably structured, or on a fairly *ad hoc* basis?
- Have you thought about conducting an audit of your present project? If so, how will you structure it, and to whom will you circulate the results?
- Finally, a test of how effective you have been as a project leader: would you like to lead another project? Will you be asked to do so? Will you be able to gain the support of your former team members for your new project?

Additional reading

- Covey, S. 1992, *The Seven Habits of Highly Effective People*, Simon & Schuster, London.

Index